SOUL
IN
MANAGEMENT

SOUL
in
Management

**How African-American
Managers Thrive in the
Competitive Corporate
Environment**

Richard F. America and Bernard E. Anderson

A Birch Lane Press Book
Published by Carol Publishing Group

To Amy
and
to Scott

A Birch Lane Press Book
Published by Carol Publishing Group
Birch Lane Press is a registered trademark of Carol Communications,
   Inc.
Editorial, sales and distribution, and rights and permissions inquiries should be
addressed to Carol Publishing, 120 Enterprise Avenue, Secaucus, N.J. 07094.

In Canada: Canadian Manda Group, One Attlantic Avenue, Suite 105, Toronto,
Ontario M6K 3E7

Carol Publishing Group books may be purchased in bulk at special discounts
for sales promotion, fund-raising, or educational purposes. Special editions can
be created to specifications. For details, contact Special Sales Department,
Carol Publishing Group, 120 Enterprise Avenue, Secaucus, N.J. 07094.

Manufactured in the United States of America
10 9 8 7 6 5 4 3 2 1

Library of Congress Cataloging-in-Publication Data

America, Richard F.
   Soul in management : how African-American managers thrive in
the competitive corporate environment / Richard F. America and
Bernard E. Anderson.
      p.   cm.
   "A Birch Lane Press book."
   ISBN 1-55972-353-X (hardcover)
   1. Afro-American executives. I. Anderson, Bernard E. II. Title.
HD38.25.U6A45   1996
658.4'09'08996073—dc20   95-50092
                                                              CIP

CONTENTS

Acknowledgments vi

Introduction vii

1. The Seven Dangerous Misconceptions 3
2. Defining Racism—and Identifying Racists 9
3. Starting Out on the Right Foot 30
4. Making the Most of Performance Appraisals 45
5. Working With Your Boss 60
6. Getting Ahead 85
7. Leading From Your Strength 107
8. Understanding the Value of Loyalty 135
9. Negotiating the Minefield of Office Politics 148
10. Socializing With Colleagues 166
11. Gaining Maturity, Emotional Growth, and Awareness 177
12. Staying in Sync With Other Black Managers 196
13. Helping the Community 212

Select Bibliography 226

Index 233

ACKNOWLEDGMENTS

This book is largely based on conversations, both structured and informal, with African-American managers over twenty years. So we first thank these men and women who shared their experiences and insights.

We also especially thank Arnold Roane, Clarence Cooper, Tom Williams, and Colleen Jones for reviewing parts of the manuscript and offering critiques and suggestions for revision.

We acknowledge outstanding editing help in turning a manuscript into a book. Our editor, Bruce Shostak; copy editor, India Cooper; and production editor, Carrie Nichols Cantor, provided the old-fashioned critique and organizational and stylistic rework that most authors need but often don't receive. Many agents, editors, and writers seem to believe this kind of excellent revision has gone out of style under the bottom-line pressure of the modern publishing industry. But great editing lives. And, needless to say, the flaws that remain are our responsibility alone. Ed Knappman has been a worthy agent, placing the book in a house where it has received enthusiastic support.

Finally, thanks to Dino Salin and Amy Salin America for helping in lots of ways.

INTRODUCTION

"Don't bother just to be better than your contemporaries or predecessors. Try to be better than yourself."

WILLIAM FAULKNER

"Get on the right track, baby."

RAY CHARLES

African-American managers, in more and more companies, have emerged as leaders, innovators, and have added value, and often become change agents in corporations ready for organizational transformation. All this has been happening at a time when many, and perhaps most, companies have been forced to restructure and adopt more-with-less strategies.

This book is primarily for African-American managers in those environments, and secondarily for all other managers who want a better grasp of these new social and cultural realities.

Soul in Management distills some of the knowledge and guidance that is being accumulated by African-American managers. Regardless of their performance, many black managers continue to face subtle, racially motivated opposition. They are still seen as threats by many associates, particularly in Old Guard companies with traditional hierarchies and command and control value systems. It's backlash behavior from these quarters that explains much of the conflict and dysfunction that's still a part of daily life in too many companies.

To manage effectively in these circumstances takes extra know-how. So one key recommendation, based on the experience of so many managers, is that black managers especially need to be life-long students of the finest thinking in the art of management, and not merely practitioners of the received wisdom about manage-ment as it happens to be understood in their company.

The book looks at the experience of black managers since the late 1970s. We formally interviewed fifty managers, and informally discussed these issues with one hundred more over a five-year period. (All names used in the book are fictitious.) It was conceived as a kind of follow-up to our 1978 book, *Moving Ahead: Black Managers in American Business*. But as it turned out, the focus is less on career strategies and how to fit in, and more on how to lead effectively, how to manage a well-balanced personal life, getting satisfaction from multiple sources, including many outside of professional life.

It also highlights the usefulness of periodic psychological coun-seling and continuing investment in personal growth, and pro-poses that all managers should routinely adopt this practice in order to function effectively in complex, multilayered organiza-tions where unconscious motivations are frequently driving be-havior and decisions, more than rational analysis and professional considerations.

The key is to focus on your own character strengths and weak-nesses, and to make steady improvements where needed. You can-not control or even greatly influence those you work with. But you can have significant control over your own behavior. So in conflict and potential conflict situations, the important thing is to detach from the opponent, and concentrate on changing your own role in whatever produced the trouble.

A further finding is that the difficulties that are now arising, as differentiated from those that arose twenty to thirty years ago, are based on the fact that many African-American managers are in sit-uations in which they have superior knowledge, skill, ability, and experience. They are objectively better. And this fact creates strong resentments and incentives to sabotage among white col-leagues and superiors who feel the status mismatch acutely. This is a turning of the tables, and it provokes all kinds of destructive dynamics unless recognized and skillfully managed.

Finally, we believe that partisan political considerations and philosophical world views largely determine the "fit" that is used to decide who gets to the top and who hits the "ceiling." The book devotes much attention to this dimension because these factors have come to determine the suitability question more than race per se.

We make two broad but useful distinctions between the kinds of corporate environments that black managers find themselves in. There are Old Guard and Vanguard companies, and black managers generally do better in the latter. Thinking generally about "business" or the "corporation" won't do. Some distinctions, however broad, have to be made.

This is not a scholarly book. It is not based on a random sample, and it does not produce statistically tested findings. Pathbreaking research of that nature is being carried out by, among others, David Thomas at Harvard Business School. He will soon be producing a book of deep scholarship on this subject. And we look forward to it eagerly.

Soul in Management approaches the subject in a style that is closer to journalism. It distills experience, and it draws heavily on a wide reading of secondary sources. Readers will be able to test their experience against those of our discussants. And they'll spot and define common problems and concerns, and draw useful lessons.

We intend the book to illuminate better ways for African-American managers to adjust to and cope with the new and still evolving dynamics of race relations in management teams.

Company Culture: How Do You Fit In?

Company culture—the overall environment you, as a manager, work in—comes in two basic types, and the kind of company you're in affects what you do and how you do it. We'll borrow some terminology from James O'Toole of the University of Southern California and ask: Are you in a *Vanguard* company or an *Old Guard* company?

According to O'Toole, Old Guard companies, although successful in many ways, concentrate too much on short-run profits and stock-market reaction. They have flawed managements and outdated concepts. Old Guard companies are hierarchical, seniority-conscious, bureaucratic, and tradition-bound. They are managed disproportionately by autocratic, Theory X types. Teledyne, Texas Instruments, GM, and ITT, among many others, are Old Guard according to O'Toole.

O'Toole's Vanguards include Levi Strauss, ARCO, John Deere, Kodak, Weyerhaeuser, Motorola, Honeywell, Dayton Hudson, and many others from many industries. Vanguards are progressive. They're less hierarchical and more likely to be in growth industries. And their management culture is more likely to tend toward collaborative Theory Z. They aren't perfect, but it happens that the Vanguards also have positive reputations as places where African-American managers are well used and well rewarded. Vision in strategy matches vision in managing race relations.

How do you fit your company culture? Smoothly or roughly? Does your company make diversity a functional reality? That means, can you help change it for the better, or are you simply expected to be grateful for being there and to go along quietly with the status quo? Half of the Fortune 500 companies have diversity programs. Does yours? Is your company's culture conducive to your growth and effectiveness? Can you improve it? If not, what will you do?

Many Fortune 1000 firms have solid reputations as good places for African-American managers. *Black Enterprise* lists them every year. For example, in 1992 these were the best companies to work for:

Ameritech	Ford	McDonald's
AT&T	Gannett	Merck
Avon	General Mills	Nynex

Chrysler	General Motors	Pepsi Cola
Coca-Cola	IBM	Philip Morris
Corning	Johnson and Johnson	TIAA-CREF
Du Pont	Kellogg's	United Airlines
Equitable	Marriott	Xerox
Federal Express		

Since 1975, we have interviewed and observed many black managers and tracked their integration in management. Based on this work, we report six basic premises:

1. If you have the right stuff, you can rise to senior management in many corporations. You have a better shot in Vanguard companies than in Old Guard firms.

2. If you have average skills—and that describes most managers—you'll be less effective and less rewarded than comparable white managers.

3. If you're technically competent but lack political or social skills and polish and the right outlook and personality for your company's specific culture, some of your white counterparts are likely to be threatened by your competence and will try to use their organizational and social ties to prevent you from implementing changes or gaining influence.

4. Injustice is a given. But you can choose to fight, complain, and remain a "victim," or finesse it and concentrate on your craft and your objectives.

5. Another key factor helps determine whether you will move to senior management. Beyond personality, style, performance, and achievement, *philosophical compatibility* matters. Loyalty, especially similar values and worldviews, including partisan politics, will determine at what point you hit the racial ceiling.

6. It is beneficial to invest time and money to become more conscious and self-aware and to commit to lifelong learning and continuing education, which can include psychological counseling, both individual and in groups. This will help you to *choose* responses consciously and focus your energies.

Effective Performance

Our review of black managers' experience suggests these guidelines for effective performance:

- Find primary satisfaction inherent in your work.
- Master the job technically and managerially.
- Keep social and status benefits and perks in perspective.
- Concentrate on performance and on being good at your craft.
- Don't participate in destructive office politics.
- Instead, develop credibility and a reputation for being consistent and technically reliable.
- Get jobs done on time, within budget, through an effective staff that's committed to you based on *mutual earned respect.*

Even if you follow this course, you'll meet injustice. For the time being, there's little you can do about that except know your rights and protect them if they're overtly or covertly threatened.

You won't lessen your anger or stress by recognizing that reality. But African-American managers will do best to concentrate on high quality and innovative performance. It's still too early in the process of mutual learning and accommodation to expect those who are your adversaries, or are suspicious of you because you're black, to drop their deeply ingrained cultural assumptions and definitions of their self-interest. Since you can't change them—though they are changing fitfully, reluctantly, unevenly, and incompletely—find your niche and do your job well. And, off the job, enjoy life's richness.

Don't Worry, Be Happy

Surveys report that black managers experience much frustration, stress, anger, and disillusionment. And at workshops and conferences, junior, middle, and senior black managers report injustices in the workplace. There's a tendency to gripe. And no wonder! But more often than not, time spent griping is wasted time. Instead, use the time to sharpen skills, make and solidify contacts, establish technical and professional credibility and self-confidence, and consolidate gains. The payoff will come after the year 2000 when critical mass has been reached in upper middle management.

The period 1970, when inroads began, to 2000 is producing a pool of well-prepared, seasoned, experienced, savvy African-American executives who will become leaders in the twenty-first century. That's the big picture. Now is the time to get ready. Don't expect instant acceptance and recognition, and under the circumstances, ten to twenty years is "instant." But you have the opportunity to study, prepare for, enter, succeed in, and enjoy managing as never before.

More and more talented black managers are leaving companies to join black-owned and -managed firms or to set up their own. Over the next ten years, black firms will grow in number and size and gain market share in mainstream service and manufacturing industries. And they'll need quality executives.

Wherever you are, these are times of scientific, financial, behavioral, political, technological, and organizational innovations and breakthroughs in many industries. Contribute to that. That's the reward in itself, *the inherent value of your work.* Choose to solve problems rather than to dwell on unfairness.

Be Aware of Issues and Obstacles

The issues facing you, as a black manager, can be summarized in these nineteen words: credibility, confidence, confrontation, culture, competence, character, choice, change, criticism, consciousness, contradiction, deference, personality, trust, insubordination, injustice, autonomy, ambivalence, loyalty. Most managers have blind spots, unconscious zones. Irrational decisions are common. But as you become more aware of your personal, social, political, and managerial motivations, you'll improve your performance and maximize your satisfaction and achievement.

You want to succeed. You work hard and smart. You've had the right education, and you keep up with your professional reading and attend the workshops like everyone else. But that's not enough. You need something extra. You need to be able to deal with doubt, opposition, and resentment, and be fully responsible for your own development, overcome ambivalence and resistance, recognize and respond to political traps, and maintain your integrity.

And to rise to senior management, you have to solve the loyalty problem: how to be a team player without having to sell your soul. Good work will take you up the rigging and into middle management. But suppose you want to make the commitment to rise further, where the leadership challenges and opportunities to produce change are greatest? Then you must make extra accommodations, lifestyle trade offs and a total commitment to the firm.

It's unrealistic to expect conservative, hierarchical, autocratic corporations to yield influence quickly to people like you, people who are perceived, often correctly, as liberal change agents. That's the nub of it. Most black managers want not only to participate (equal opportunity) but also to change things. And there's usually natural resistance from the organization.

Three clusters of issues spark conflict and motivate others to try to impede your performance and career growth:

- uncertainty about your loyalties
- differences in personality, style, values, and habits of mind
- reactions to your nonstereotypical, competent, and threateningly high-quality performance, innovative ideas, and leadership ability

To that end, management advisers often give you this advice:

- Be honest and open in communication.
- Delegate, trust, and encourage group decisions.
- Encourage your staff to be creative.
- Don't manage too closely.
- Manage by objectives.
- Support and treat people as individuals.

- Listen actively.
- Concentrate on quality.

That's fine as far as it goes. But what about race, which has a powerful influence on business performance? You can reduce race as a barrier to effectiveness, and sometimes you can make it work for you.

In the future, many managers who work well with people will outperform others of greater technical skill. That's because organizations will be more complex and staffs more diverse. And strong leadership and interpersonal skills will produce better results.

It appears that proportionately more white managers are Theory X (authoritarian) and more black managers are Theory Y (trusting, noncontrolling), but that may reflect generational factors more than race or culture. It further seems likely that Theory Y and Theory Z (team-oriented, consensual, participative) will be styles that better meet organizational needs of the future. This book will help you better understand authority and power in interracial settings and avoid mistakes that produce conflicts, ruin projects, and sidetrack careers.

Lateral moves are increasingly common within flatter-matrix organizations. You can move from being the outsider to being an accepted, effective member or leader.

Without trauma or race-based resistance, you can:

- manage with confidence
- win cooperation
- deal with hostility and sabotage without losing your dignity
- open and maintain communication
- grow and enjoy your work
- maintain self-respect and your own perspective

The ideas in this book can also help you:

- recruit, retain, and inspire quality staff
- cut absenteeism and lift morale

- improve output and product and service quality
- consistently meet or exceed your objectives
- inspire peer and superior confidence
- increase your credibility, sociability, marketability, and mobility
- reduce resentment, hostility, isolation, and alienation
- meet subordinates' and bosses' needs and keep their loyalty

The Lessons

1. Know what manager type and what personality type you are.

2. Many white managers are ambivalent about you. When you have problems, first check your own sins of omission or commission before blaming others or racism. Understand racism and how to deal with it effectively.

3. Be responsible for your career.

4. Get consistent, useful performance feedback and appraisal.

5. Support your boss's aspirations. But when you have a poor fit, don't stagnate. Have an agenda. Find a new job or lateral reassignment.

6. Establish a specialty and earn people's confidence in it.

7. Study leadership and strive to be a good leader as well as a good manager.

8. Know where you stand ideologically, and find an organization where you can be philosophically comfortable.

9. Cultivate your networks.

10. Learn to deal with emotions triggered on the job, especially anger and disappointment.

11. Help other black managers.

12. Use your position to help the community.

Those lessons can help you increase effectiveness, rewards, and satisfaction. But whether your career has been smooth or bumpy, your firm's culture can present traps and dead-ends not clearly marked. No matter how friendly your colleagues, your situation can be perilous, especially in an Old Guard company. Situations can turn sour when slights and collisions accumulate. So find and trust the reliable people. Fortunately there are many of them—and more all the time.

Draw Your Own Conclusions

This book is not a report of complaints. Instead, it is a tool to help you, as part of a pioneering generation of African-American managers, emerge as an excellent leader of a quality organization. Quality management is a high calling and a fine art. So savor the artistry.

There is a large popular and academic literature on management, full of how-to-do-everything books and articles, and we refer to it and draw on it in each of this book's chapters. Magazines like *Forbes*, *Fortune*, *Black Enterprise*, and *Business Week* that cover professional conduct and career strategy were valuable secondary sources. The *New York Times*, *Washington Post*, and *Philadelphia Inquirer* consistently feature excellent columns on life and work that were useful throughout, especially in chapter 5 on relations with superiors and in chapter 11 on emotional expression.

Each chapter includes comments from our interview subjects. We address concerns, issues raised, and lessons that can be drawn. In doing so, we draw on ideas from many sources and consider many concepts that, in a broad sense, apply to any manager but especially to the situations faced by black managers.

This book is, in some ways, like a business-school case. There are no right or wrong answers.

But it's for you to draw conclusions that fit your circumstances and personality. There are no universal solutions to these evolving problems. Make conscious choices based on the costs and benefits of proceeding as you have been or by making sometimes difficult changes.

Another Way to Look at It

Finally, here's another way to summarize the key lessons for achievement, survival, and growth that will emerge in various contexts throughout the book:

1. *Let it pass.* Don't worry over minor irritations, slights, and differences in style.

2. *Look objectively at your own performance.* You'll often find you contributed to your own problems and conflicts. Disciplined self-criticism is crucial to improve your surviving and thriving skills.

3. *Keep your eye on the prize.* Always remember that old hymn and civil rights anthem. Know your objectives, add value, and don't let distractions sidetrack you.

4. *Absorb and leave.* Develop credibility, skills, contacts, experience, and a record of achievements to take with you to your own business, some other black-owned business, or any other business that offers you a bona fide opportunity in a hospitable, unconstrained environment.

5. *Know that success is the best revenge.* Don't brook or nurse grudges and fantasies of revenge by getting even on your adversary's terms. Instead, live by the preceding four lessons, and your ultimate success will cause your opponents more heartburn than any organizational gambit can.

6. *Maintain the absence of desire.* This directive is borrowed from Zen. You'll find greater harmony and well-being by *not* striving, in the Western sense of grasping, consuming ambition. Pursue excellence for its own intrinsic value, and the inner satisfaction will be reward enough.

Look Toward the Way It Will Be

This book reports experience at entry, middle, and senior levels, in industries as diverse as aerospace research, chemicals, office equipment, and financial services. We talk with managers at IBM, General Electric, Xerox, Hewlett Packard, Martin-Lockheed, Ford, McKinsey, Booz Allen, Bankers Trust, Bechtel,

Levi Strauss, Coopers and Lybrand, the Washington Post Company, Arthur Andersen, and Unysis, among others.

There were 150,000 to 300,000 of you—African-American managers—in 1996. Some problems you face are classic and universal. Others are widely experienced but complicated by race. Some are uniquely yours. Keep in mind, though, that black and white managers have many common strengths, weaknesses, dreams, fears, fantasies, and unconscious conflicts. Much of what happens that might seem racially motivated and hostile only reflects individual failings, lack of information, and anxiety.

Still, you face challenges and uncertainties unknown to most white managers. You're under extra pressure to perform. And you may feel excluded from channels of informal communication and separated from peers by differences in background, attitudes, perceptions of the environment, and, in some cases, personal values and beliefs.

Affirmative action stimulates wider opportunities. But it can also cause problems of adjustment, because many people—superiors, peers, subordinates, clients, and customers—believe, or say they believe, that you are not as qualified as someone else who could have gotten your job.

A barrier to top jobs also exists, as we've seen, because of doubts about your loyalty and visceral commitment to all corporate goals, including social goals and goals that are fundamentally political. But white managers also feel unappreciated, bypassed, unrecognized, underchallenged, overworked, oppressed, insecure, and shaky to some degree, some of the time. You're not alone. And race doesn't explain it all. Everybody has problems.

SOUL
IN
MANAGEMENT

1

The Seven Dangerous Misconceptions

"Nothing astonishes men as much as common sense and plain dealing."

RALPH WALDO EMERSON

"I'm beginning to see the light."

DUKE ELLINGTON

African-American managers seem prone to accept seven fundamental misconceptions about race in the corporate environment. Unfortunately, they just confuse the issue. Here they are:

1. Corporate self-interest will reduce discrimination and lead to fairness.

2. Ceilings will be removed if you complain.

3. Your job is simply to manage, not to be an agent of social change.

4. The proper professional response to injustice and offense is direct confrontation.

5. The likely future course of race relations is static.

6. A career is a ladder to be climbed.

7. You have to be twice as good, or at least better, to do as well as white managers.

What's wrong with these seven points?

1. Corporate self-interest should reduce discrimination and lead to fairness.

It's often asserted by academics, journalists, and senior managers that corporations should remove racial ceilings and should practice affirmative action because the status quo wastes talent and is bad for the company and bad for the country. It's certainly true that wasting talent is bad for your employer and for society. But the way this is usually presented is based on a shaky assumption: that merely pointing this out will be constructive and will change behavior.

That's unlikely, because those white managers who still discriminate in assignments, rewards, and promotions don't define what's good for the company or country the same way you define it. They want to maintain the racial status quo or even turn back black advances made so far. You can see that clearly by reading between the lines of many conservative corporate commentators in *Forbes*, *Fortune*, and the *Wall Street Journal*, arguing against affirmative action and "preferences." So, calling for justice by arguing that it's in the self-interest of those who perpetuate injustice won't work. They don't agree that what you prefer is in their self-interest. They decide their own self-interest, not even the interest of the company. And it's based on maximizing their personal advantages over you—individual and group, economic and noneconomic.

It's naive and useless to appeal to their presumed rational motives and ask them to play fair "because it pays." They don't think it pays. The message falls on deaf ears. And sending it demeans you, because it comes from weakness and supplication. The premise that discriminators really only hurt themselves and would be better off accepting diversity may be true, but you'll never convince the discriminators. Don't waste time and energy trying.

2. Ceilings will be removed if you complain.

You hear a lot about ceilings. The popular sense is that black managers seldom get beyond middle management. And racism explains this blockage.

A better view is this: Yes, there seems to be a ceiling. But it's higher than it was ten years ago. It will be higher ten years from now. But there will still be an upper limit on aspirations and advancement, especially in Old Guard companies.

Black managers and business writers complain about such limits. But what's fair has nothing to do with it. Corporations are political, social, and cultural institutions. So don't expect entrenched managers to step aside to let people who seem different in outlook gain influence and authority and implement changes.

There *will* be breakthroughs. The ceiling will shift upward. But most black managers must face up, ship out, or accept ceiling situations. So work smart. Gain technical expertise. Become a knowledgeable, skilled manager and leader. Add value. Get a track record. Develop contacts and networks. And then choose where you want to be, where you want to go.

You can choose to accept the ceiling and find satisfaction intrinsically in your tasks, or leave and go where there's a more hospitable, open culture and political environment, which more and more often means going to black-owned and -managed businesses. If that turns out to be the case, then ceilings in the Fortune 1000 may unwittingly help accelerate development of large, competitive African-American firms by diverting much of the best talent to their offices.

Indeed, for black managers part of the solution to the problem of career impediments is the emergence of stronger black businesses. These will increasingly offer challenging, rewarding opportunities. And they will be instruments of broad social and political change, as well as community development, in ways most Fortune 1000 firms can't be.

3. Your job is simply to manage, not to be an agent of social change.

Why are you in management? This is not some existential

trick question. Instead, it gets to your motivation for being a manager rather than a teacher, preacher, lawyer, doctor, engineer, scientist, or entrepreneur. As a black manager, you have various economic and intellectual motivations. But, given the history of civil rights, one of those should be your desire to see broad social change, and management offers you a base, a platform, and an environment in which to work, directly and indirectly, for progressive change.

The civil rights movement is still moving forward, and you should be part of it. The question is, how effective can you be? If you've not thought of it this way, you have lots of company. But being a manager gives you tools and opportunities to create and introduce social and political changes, if you choose to.

Such considerations are far from the minds of most managers. But you have a historic obligation. If you're not doing what you can to promote change, you're wasting an opportunity. Rethink what you're about. Many unheralded people paid a price so you could be where you are. You have a collective and individual obligation to make a conscious difference.

4. The proper professional response to injustice and offense is direct confrontation.

Occasionally you have to deal with organizational injustice. The source may be someone's conscious decision or the inertia and mindless, irrational workings of bureaucratic systems and processes. Either way, decide when to accept and flow with it and when to confront.

Zen Buddhism and other Eastern philosophies emphasize nondirected resistance, which is letting opponents' power work against them. Whether it's an individual or the system, it's usually best not to confront. Instead, let aggressors defeat themselves by clumsily trying to apply inappropriate or excessive force against you. That means you should sidestep most office assaults. Don't be drawn in. Sidestepping someone who is out to cause you problems saves you energy, which you can focus on objectives rather than on a pointless contest you did not plan or originate.

You can manage, lead, make a difference, get rewards, recognition, and satisfaction, lead a balanced life, and not sell your soul. Be confident of your ability, not only to perform but also to innovate and to influence changes. You can be tough-minded, compete with the best, and still be concerned with human relations, community affairs, and corporate social responsibility.

5. The likely future course of race relations is static.

General social dynamics affect what happens in your organization. One of those is race relations, and they are not static. For forty years there has been change, and shifts will continue. But much discussion of race and management assumes the future will be a straight-line extrapolation of the past, either flat or at the same rate of change. That's not likely.

Situations you face ten or twenty years from now will be influenced by complex factors, including the racial climate of the time. But we too often base our expectations about the indefinite future on current and recent past experience. That's a mistake. Anticipate change—and remain flexible, because there will be surprises, good and bad.

6. A career is a ladder to be climbed.

Climbing the ladder is not the right imagery for most managers, including black managers. Neither is moving up the pyramid. Career paths are not straight up and down. What happens is more like climbing a ship's rigging. There are many lateral moves, and the process is not rigid, as ladder-imagery suggests. It's constantly shifting. It's loose, flexible, unstable. You hang on and move up or sideways as best you can. And it gets narrower near the top. Simultaneously, other people are moving laterally. And some are even coming down as you go up.

7. You have to be twice as good, or at least better, to do as well as white managers.

The assertion that you must be twice as good as white managers to get the same rewards, recognition, and respect is repeated in workshops, conferences, books, and casual conversation. How has such a baseless notion persisted?

The average black manager has the same smarts and talent as the average white manager. In any organization, given its formal and informal arrangements and culture, managers of the same basic ability work at about the same intensity. There will be variations—for example, some managers will be workaholics—but most managers work about equally hard. The average black manager won't outwork the average white manager. So being "twice as good" is meaningless rhetoric. It's a myth that persists unexamined and unchallenged.

Where you, as a black manager, can get an edge is in consciousness and awareness. By working to be more conscious of yourself and of your environment, and by paying attention to your own and others' emotional state, you can gain an advantage, because most managers, for personal and cultural reasons, are unconscious, unreflective, and unaware. You can choose to become more aware and can outperform these competitors in environments where these qualities are recognized and rewarded. You must work smarter, not harder.

If you develop these insights and skills, you'll succeed where others blunder, generate turmoil, and lower performance and productivity. You can choose how to react and how and when to be proactive. But to choose, you have to be aware, conscious, and thinking. To become aware of your inner states and of office dynamics, *work* to be aware.

Race *is* important. But in most companies, personality is more important. How you fare will depend most on how you present yourself in everyday life. Your personality will have more to do with how you cope and how you influence your circumstances than racial dynamics will. In this sense, the significance of race has declined. There was a time, not long ago, when race was always the dominant factor.

2

Defining Racism—
and Identifying Racists

"There is no prejudice that the work of art does not finally overcome."

ANDRÉ GIDE

"Ebony and Ivory live together in perfect harmony."

STEVIE WONDER AND
PAUL MCCARTNEY

Racism can influence your entry-level, training, junior, middle, and even senior management experience. And it can emerge at any time, anywhere in your career.

The standard social science definition of racism is as follows: a doctrine of racial differences in character and intelligence, inherent superiority, and the practice of discrimination, segregation, persecution, and domination. But that's not adequate. It won't help you address many professional situations. It doesn't cover the kinds of attitudes and behavior common in business.

Dictionary Racism

Since there's so much preoccupation with the word *racism* and its impact, let's start by thinking through what we really mean by it and how it can be more useful. We think about racism carelessly. In popular use, the term includes mere race consciousness—behaving positively or negatively toward people according to their race, discriminating. If Susan so much as notices race, that's somehow "racist." She's supposed to be color-blind. But that's not a useful practical definition. And personal hostilities between people of different races are not necessarily motivated by racism.

Racism is the belief that one's race is superior and therefore has a right to dominate. It's expressed in many ways. But you can only surmise that underlying attitude exists. You can't prove it's there. As a practical matter, there are two types of racism: *personal racism* and *policy racism*. (We also speak of *institutional racism*, but that is actually policy racism, institutionalized in tradition and practice.) Most managers whose personal beliefs are racist are sophisticated enough to conceal it, but many pursue racist objectives by adopting politically "conservative" policy positions. In other words, within the corporate culture racism can be given socially acceptable expression in policy preference. It's an indirect, oblique strategy, and it's often couched in terms of high principle, moral authority, and concern for the nation's and the company's interest.

This doesn't mean that all political conservatives are racists—far from it—but there is a high correlation between conservatism and racism. Some conservative managers base their positions on principle, arrived at through honest intellectual analysis. But others are largely motivated by personal beliefs about society and race. Usually, conservative managers want to restrict and minimize government intervention and regulation, especially in race-related matters, such as equal employment and housing opportunity, educational spending, and business development and procurement programs. They oppose affirmative action and set-asides, what they would call preferences, and quotas, for instance. But that's usually code language for their general hostility to any further changes that might alter the status quo on race, no matter how they're pursued, privately or at government's initiative.

A Practical View of Racism

First of all, don't fret about slights and the common, ordinary bumps and bruises of corporate life. These are often interpreted as racially motivated, but usually they're just ambitious or insensitive human beings colliding, having an accident. Don't be paranoid, argumentative, accusatory, or blaming. Try not to have a chip on your shoulder. These are common and probably normal responses to the competitive give and take, but they waste time.

Instead, take a practical approach to thinking about managerial racism. Here are its key elements:

1. Behavior in which managers react to someone based on race, positively or negatively, usually the latter, is racism. Racism is not simply prejudice or discrimination, although they *are* part of it, of course. If you see the pattern of a double standard in decisions, assignments, performance appraisals, or rewards, then probably you're seeing racism.

2. Racism is in the eye of the beholder. It's a matter of subjective probability, an intuitive judgment based on subtle patterns. You alone decide who is racist. No one has to agree with you or admit anything. You get a hunch that Harry is racist. The hunch is based on cues you notice. Often you see that double standard, but blatant, open, aggressive, hostile discrimination is risky. And it's rare.

3. Ordinarily, you can't prove racism. There's no third party, no arbitrator, panel, or judge, to determine objectively whether someone, some subtle behavior, or an adverse decision is racist. Of course, there are Equal Employment Opportunity (EEO), and Office of Contract Compliance (OFCCP) laws and regulations, complaint procedures, hearings, investigations, and findings. But those have to do with overt disparate treatment or impact, or with "statistical discrimination." What you are more likely to encounter— the use of administrative discretion to hurt you—won't generally lend itself to such formal and legalistic procedures.

4. The label "racist" is useless when it's tossed around as an accusation. Forget about making, in the commonly heard phrase, "charges of racism." Instead, when you get "the hunch," think of it as a working assumption for your private practical benefit. It's based on signals and clues that you alone process and on your knowledge of the way things work in our society. It's a judgment you make to protect yourself when you've noticed a pattern of actions or comments warning that you're dealing with someone who will try to block you or diminish you in some way, directly or indirectly, actively or passively.

Working With Racists

When you're in a conflict, look first at yourself to understand why. Often you'll find you have contributed, by commission or omission. Racism may be a factor. But acknowledge your own error. That's key. This attitude will make you more diligent, less complaining, less stressed, and more effective.

You can work with racists while minimizing the impact of racism. You do that by strong performance and by being aware of, and learning to manage and deal with, your own shortcomings. Of course, it helps if you have the personality of the born diplomat and can let things roll off your back. But many of us can't do that. So we have to work at it.

It usually does no good to confront a person you believe is a racist. Your accusation would inevitably be denied. And then what have you accomplished? The resentment would lead to some kind of retaliation, direct or indirect, sooner or later. Then relations will deteriorate further. And Harry has friends who can cause you trouble, too. So what should you do?

The Benefit of the Doubt

Begin relationships with white colleagues by assuming each is a *Neutral*. Neutrals will not show any particular signs of either racial feeling or of instant rapport and reliability. You won't be able to peg them as leaning toward you or against you. You won't get an immediate reading on their politics or social views. Most managers present themselves as decent, regular professionals. They're trying to do their jobs, get on in this world, and handle their own problems as best they can. It's only after exposure and interaction, especially when there are significant stakes, that you pick up clues that some are not Neutrals.

Some Neutrals turn out to be *Solids*, good people. They make good personal friends as well as colleagues. They are often socially aware. And they can be courageous and reliable in a showdown situation on a matter of principle. They are often true-blue. Indeed, they can be more trustworthy and helpful than many of your black colleagues. And, fortunately, more and more managers are Solids.

Unfortunately, some others are racists. However, it does little good to simply decide Harry is racist, because the term covers a great range of attitude and behavior. Not only are there personal and policy racists, there are, as we'll see, at least six types of policy racists. Collect enough experiential data in dealing with Harry to make a judgment. Be fair. Don't make snap judgments in anger after one incident or disagreement. Wait to see if a pattern emerges.

Of course, listen to other black managers' assessments. What do they think? But reserve judgment. Draw your own firsthand conclusions. "Racism" is often an unfair, inaccurate label. It can arise out of incidents that are merely personal and not racially motivated. Used loosely, it is slander. So don't toss an accusation of racism around lightly. Discount it when you hear it from just one source. But if it comes from two independent, reliable sources, with no obvious axes to grind, give it some credence.

Once you have sufficient clues and evidence, if you conclude Harry is racist, determine in your mind his level of racism. This step is usually missing, we overgeneralize, and that's why the way we usually think about racism has little practical value in business. This exercise helps you sort out the clues and signals you think you've detected. Then you're prepared to deal with Harry more effectively.

Levels of Racism

We assume most managers share the prevailing attitudes of society about race. So, as a practical matter, under certain competitive circumstances many managers will reveal themselves as personal and policy racists. The question is, *how* racist?

Racism is often the word used to describe Harry's insensitivity and inability or lack of motivation to pay attention to African-American associates' sensibilities. Managers perceived as racist are frequently criticized for this. They're said to "lack consciousness" and to be "insensitive" to issues of justice and equity. And that's because they had no personal contact and education on the subject in their formative years.

But there's a more useful way to view it. Insensitivity and lack of awareness is not the important point. Most racists are aware of their feelings and attitudes toward you. They may be inconsistent. They may feel ambivalent or guilty. And they may modify their assumptions, attitudes, and actions over time, based on experience, training, and reflection. They learn to deal with reality. Fortunately, racist beliefs can be unlearned.

But until they are, racists will believe that in intelligence, creativity, spirituality, morality, productivity, and virtue, their race is inherently superior to yours. Therefore they believe that they are superior to you. That belief produces feelings of entitlement. Racists believe that they and "people like them" are entitled to dominate you and "people like you" and to enjoy disproportionate shares of income, wealth, influence, leadership, and privilege. Many seem to think they are entitled also to extra deference and respect.

Racists base their social, political, economic, and managerial decisions on these beliefs and feelings. It's not just that they don't like you or would prefer to avoid you or to limit your access, influence, impact, recognition, and rewards. They feel entitled to outrank you, to have their analyses, judgments, recommendations, and decisions accorded greater weight, to discount you, to enjoy advantages over you, and to have you defer to them.

How strong are these attitudes? That's a key factor in how integrated management and professional teams function. Many black managers believe most white managers want to monopolize privilege and power. This contributes to conflict when black managers aspire to compete and lead, especially when you want to change the way the unit operates or change some policy.

There are degrees of racism beyond the basic attitude of superiority and entitlement. But before we elaborate, let's emphasize this point: your company has plenty of managers you can work with. Almost all of them are Neutrals at the outset of your relationship. And most will work with you smoothly 90 percent of the time.

The problem is, crunch time will come around: when there's a sensitive decision, a choice assignment, or a question of whose recommendation to follow, whose judgment to rely on, whose analysis to believe. At crunch time, the decision-making process is most likely to become weighted with racial factors. And when underlying attitudes clash, relationships deteriorate, and Neutrals may reveal themselves to be racists. This book, in many ways, is about how to deal with that tough 10 percent of the time. Those instances cumulatively make or break careers.

Crunch time is when the concept of levels of racism becomes applicable. Then, a manager who is initially a Neutral becomes defined in your mind more clearly.

Level 1. Purgers. They are the extreme. They believe the black presence in the United States is acceptable as long as African Americans are economically productive but politically passive. Purgers would support policies restricting black political participation and stifling, expelling, or deporting activist "troublemakers." Purgers include some ideologically conservative managers. They are the American counterpart of the hard-line South African defenders of apartheid. They will often misuse legitimate management tools, assignments, performance appraisal, and disciplinary procedures to harass and intimidate.

Level 2. Retrogressives. They don't want to suppress or rid the country of black activists, but they do want to maintain their own general and organizational advantages and the current distribution of income, wealth, position, and status. They would roll back many of the social changes made in the past thirty years. They are strict constructionists, a stance that allows them to appear principled while advancing supremacist positions. But many nevertheless support and help individual black achievers—for example, a Clarence Thomas—whom they see as useful exceptions to their negative beliefs about African Americans in general. Many senior executives are Retros.

Level 3. Ambivalents. These are also political conservatives, but they don't flatly or reflexively oppose moves toward equality in social relations. They are, instead, ambivalent: they don't want much more "socially engineered" change, but they would agree that some changes made in the past thirty years have been beneficial and fair and also serve their needs by contributing to social stability.

They are not egalitarian and are highly conscious of the personal and group advantages they have in the status quo. They believe in inherent racial superiority and feel no guilt about that. They don't care strongly whether you like or trust them. But arm's-length dealings with them can be satisfactory and businesslike. Ambivalents include many middle managers and technical professionals. Most people who identify themselves as "conservatives" are probably Ambivalents.

Level 4. Resenters. They used to be progressive allies of African-American activism, but they've had a change of heart since the late 1960s. Now they resent black assertiveness.

Resenters are angry about specific public and private incidents and personal insults they've experienced. They have become reactionary and punitive on public and corporate policy. But because of their early-life experiences and, in many cases, their elite education and enlightened self-image, they still are progressive on some social questions.

These are the neoconservatives and some neoliberals. Resenters disproportionately include people who work in the knowledge industries, especially journalists, policy analysts, and academics. Resenters provide much of the intellectual cover for Purgers and Retrogressives. They are especially concerned about "quotas," "multiculturalism," and "merit." They try to make a distinction between policies designed to achieve "equal opportunity" and those aimed at "equal outcomes," claiming to favor the former.

They, too, privately believe in inherent racial superiority, but they're conflicted on this and other complex social matters. Like Ambivalents, they aren't sure how much change is enough. They feel the need for "scientific" support before committing themselves to restrictive policy, but once they have it, they can be vociferous in their opposition to change.

Level 5. Avoiders. They include many traditional liberals and neoliberals. They share some characteristics and desires with Resenters, but they're not prepared to oppose change. They seem to feel more guilt about their shifting views and hardening attitudes, so many have turned inward since the 1960s. They're now working on personal concerns of self-actualization and self-expression, often through faddish therapies and escapist hobbies. They seek escape from social-policy complexity and from previous commitments to social change. Avoiders are often in personal or philosophical transition. Therefore, some can be inconsistent and give mixed or conflicting signals.

Level 6. Shallows. People who fall into this category tend to be good-natured, friendly, socially unaware, and largely apolitical. They don't have strong prejudices, but neither have they thought much about complex social realities. Shallows can make good working associates. But their lack of depth and social perception limits their value as allies in any conflict involving an issue of principle. These are the fraternity boys. Shallows have been known to become offensive and obnoxious in social situations, and when they are feeling uninhibited their basic racial hostilities surface.

You can work effectively with anyone of any type if you are alert, not overly sensitive, and aware of whom you're dealing with. But remember, name calling is pointless. The label "racist" insults even when all the specifications fit. Don't waste time and energy trying to stick it on someone for all to see. Instead, note individual behavior and make a private judgment. Jane has, on occasion, behaved or spoken like a racist; Susan never has. Jane seems to have a double standard; Susan doesn't. Think of your hunches about racism as working assumptions or conclusions drawn from observed behavior and from expressed or inferred political and policy attitudes. Then use them as the basis for action, if necessary.

It's usually futile and counterproductive to call anyone a racist. But there are instances and special situations of clear disparate treatment when it may help. It can raise consciousness and give useful feedback about offensive behavior. It can let Jane know you pick up clues, vibes, and signals that could spell trouble. But, generally, deal with Jane or Harry in some businesslike way. Avoid casual contact. Be tactful. Be correct. Stick to the main point. Complaining and name calling are unprofessional and unproductive, no matter the provocation.

The word *racism* is of little use to you as a charge or an indictment, even though the media carelessly use it that way. It's *your* judgment. It's unilateral, because there's no way to prove private motives and beliefs in these matters. Inference is all that's available. Denial and counterattack would follow any discussion that made your hunch explicit. So discussion is usually pointless.

Many—and in some Vanguard companies, *most*—of your white colleagues and associates are Solids. They are good people. Their values, principled commitments to honorable dealings, and integrity are beyond question. Many came out of the sixties and seventies with activist records in social justice, peace, environmental, and other movements for a better world. Some have paid some dues in your behalf.

It's lucky for you there are so many good people to work with, because otherwise there would be no way to have a realistic hope of leading and achieving. You'd always be watching your flank and looking over your shoulder. The back stabbers, idea stealers, and credit grabbers would make it hard to succeed.

Most people you first encounter as Neutrals are prepared to co-operate and accept you professionally. The trouble comes when conflict over a procedure or concept arises or when the risks of a business step to be taken arouse latent fears about your compe-tence and judgment. These fears, of course, are based on stereo-types. But that doesn't make the issue one of evil intent. It's a human issue of insecurity and risk aversion. It surfaces when the stakes rise, when your approach or presence threatens your asso-ciates' assumptions. And when you want to change something.

Stars, Old Boys, and Yammies

In general, your white colleagues, superiors, and subordinates fall into three other broad categories. These reflect their general attitudes toward organizational life.

Stars are outstanding. They're heads-up and widely admired. They're professionals. Watch their performance closely. Profes-sionally and technically, they should be your role models. Stars will generally go far and accomplish much.

Old Boys are the stereotypical, organization-centered bureau-cratic managers. They defend the status quo. They are the source of much of your trouble or potential trouble. And there are both liberal and conservative Old Boys—and Old Girls.

Yammies are a particular kind of Young, often overly Aggressive, Ambitious, Antagonistic, and usually Amoral Manager. Yammies are often quite effective. But their approach to office politics is the issue. They tend to be "out for number one" to a distasteful degree. And, unfortunately, many are ruthless: they steal ideas for which they take credit, and are back-stabbing and double-dealing. And they will, at the same time, slap your back, laugh at your jokes, and smile as if they were your friend. Watch them!

Variety Among African-American Managers

Black managers can be usefully categorized according to the degree of trust, political game playing, activism, and savvy they display. These would be applied to all managers, but for our purposes we find these distinctions useful in sorting out observed behavior and opinions expressed, because they highlight the black manager's relationship to the organization.

Trust. Some black managers are hard-liners who seem to trust nobody. Cynical and tough-minded, they see the work environment as a kind of jungle. They often talk in military metaphors. Life for them is a competition in which their colleagues are out to get them.

Those at the other end of the continuum are cordial and cooperative. They minimize the competitive aspects of daily life. They trust that their positive attitudes will be repaid in kind, that their organization is fair, and that their talents and contributions will be fairly recognized. They want to be accepted, and they often try to ingratiate themselves.

Most African-American managers probably are in the middle, alternating between feelings of mistrust and cooperation. They are not inclined to be either too hopeful or too cynical. They try to remain reality-focused. They recognize that they will encounter hostilities and need to be ready. But they also believe goodwill generates cooperation, generally.

Political game playing. This approach to categorizing black managers is borrowed from Michael Maccoby's book, *The Gamesman.* He creates four types: Jungle Fighters, Gamesmen (Gamers), Company Men (Companyers), and Craftsmen (Crafters). (We'll use the gender-neutral forms in parentheses.) Organizational style is the basis for these distinctions as well as for our other typologies.

- *Jungle Fighters* engage in intrigue and believe in survival of the fittest, and *Gamers* believe in survival of the cleverest.
- *Companyers* expect the firm to take care of their career interests in return for loyalty.
- *Crafters* concentrate on performance, study the art of management, and get satisfaction from growth as professional managers.

Perhaps you believe jungle fighting and gamesmanship are required. You obviously need political skills. But consistent performance, technical knowledge, and value added will give you the best chance of having a well-balanced and satisfying life and of preserving your integrity and your soul.

Activism. To describe black managers according to activism, we might ask: How sensitive to social and political issues are they? How committed to their beliefs? How do they use the resources they control or influence to achieve community-development objectives or to change internal social policy? They range from inactive to highly active and can be grouped into five types.

- *Unconscious* types see no obligation or opportunity to use their position to produce such benefits.
- *Lip Servers* say they see a role and look for chances to help, but their record is unconvincing.
- *Prudents* act when there's a chance to do some good with minimum personal risk. But their prime concern is to meet corporate objectives and remain always in good standing personally with their immediate superiors.
- *Pressers* are also concerned with risks and rewards, meeting unit objectives, good personal relationships, and being perceived as loyal. But they are more ideological and less inclined to accept an employer's claims of good faith. So they apply more internal pressure.
- *Bodacious* types are what used to be called Race Men or Nationalists. They see themselves as activists first. Concern for the company is secondary. Indeed, this small group might belong

among Ralph Nader's whistle blowers. They would gladly see the employer in court. They are bold and audacious activists within the company on issues like employee rights, equal employment, the environment, consumer protection and other equity matters.

Savvy. In addition to trust, political game playing, and activism, we can categorize African-American managers according to how savvy they are. How confident and professionally sophisticated do they seem? Demeanor, bearing, presence, even charisma are important. The savvy that black managers project, along with their technical competence, determines their effectiveness. This savvy scale borrows its terminology from sports.

- *Blue Chips* project high confidence, competence, and savvy. They have better than a 70 percent chance to reach senior management.
- *High Drafts*, with slightly less of these intangible qualities, have a 30 percent chance. They'll likely plateau at high middle management unless they develop their weaker characteristics.
- *Low Drafts* will plateau as middle managers or mid-level professional specialists.
- *Free Agents* will make adequate but undistinguished contributions in middle-management line jobs or slide into relatively unimportant staff jobs by mid-career or sooner.

Let's face it. Most managers of all races and genders are Free Agents. But they can get more satisfaction from work and from life as Crafters than as Gamers, Jungle Fighters, or Companyers.

The Modes and How They View Racism

Another useful way of looking at variety among black managers is according to their attitudes toward the management and organizational issues raised in the interviews we conducted. Of course, as in most human activities, in management people sometimes say one thing and do another, shift opinions over time, or simply don't know where they stand. But we have done our best to sort out the managers' attitudes in ways that make practical sense.

Black managers, like everybody else, operate and think in different *modes*, which we classified along a continuum from conservative to liberal labeled *Modes 1, 2, and 3.*

Modes are flexible and dynamic. You can be in Mode 1 on one issue and in Mode 2 or 3 on others. And you can move from one to another mode over time on any one issue. You're not locked in. But the concept allows you to peg yourself and others in a way that can clarify in your own mind where you stand.

In our interviews, we tried to get a reading on both how the managers themselves saw each issue and how they thought other black managers saw the same issue. On the role of racism in work, the modes range this way:

Mode 1 managers see racism as having little or no effect on them. Modes 2 and 3 see more. And Mode 1 places greatest emphasis on "self-help" and discipline. Their rhetorical style is strong, and there is an ideological fervor in their statements. This is the black conservative.

Mode 2 managers see racism as a more important and pervasive factor, but they focus on the ways it can be finessed, avoided, and overcome. They point to the role of personal preparation, application, dedication, and performance in producing personal and group progress.

Mode 3 managers put much greater weight on obstacles posed by systemic racism, which they see as deep-seated. They share the view that individuals *can* succeed, but they insist that active opposition is conscious and targeted and that enmity and personal hidden agendas explain much of the behavior of whites within organizations. So they believe that concerted group responses and formal, official remedies, not just individual effort, are necessary to overcome that opposition.

For the sake of ease of recall concerning these labels of style, values, and behavior, let's further refer to the three modes according to long-established philosophical distinctions that are well recognized among black people. Let's have Mode 1 be *assimilationists*, Mode 2 be *accomodationists*, and Mode 3 be *separatists*. (They are not separatists in any formal political sense, but in the sense that they are more emotionally and personally distant than modes 1 and 2 from the prevailing point of view in most companies, which are Old Guard.) Obviously these are not hard and fast distinctions. There are no pure types. We all have elements of each in our thinking. But the typology has a rough usefulness and accuracy.

What You Can Do

Understand the Political Background

To understand conflicts at work, you must understand the larger, underlying contest. Office problems are not merely organizational or personal. Class, gender, and ethnic conflicts about how to share the sociopolitical pie contribute to strife on the job.

African-American managers have to be diligent and protect themselves. Meanwhile, white managers either adapt to demographic and cultural changes—diversity—or try to resist. You're both making difficult adjustments, a process that needs time and mutual goodwill to work. But the same process leads to conflicts: over scarce resources and political influence, or maybe just between people.

At the foundation of such immediate personal, technical, and organizational issues lie these broader ones: Who fits where? And who is entitled to what? That's what we see when political phenomena like David Duke and Pat Buchanan arise, to heighten fears and insecurities over status and personal finances.

The broader struggle involves a "zero sum game" (advance at your expense) as economists express it. It's redistributive. There are winners and losers. How to divide the pie, even if it's growing? We try to pretend there are ways to accelerate African Americans' advancement without disturbing relative racial shares. But we can't do that without ample growth. And there are no prospects for such growth in the near to medium term.

So until there is another cycle of high investment and innovation, perhaps ten or even twenty years from now, modest, non-inflationary growth, at best, is all we can expect. And even with that, the question is the same: Who gets what? More provocatively, who is entitled to what? It becomes an issue of justice and equity.

Disagreement over broad public and corporate policy issues contributes to the systemic kind of racial conflict in organizations that Mode 3s talk about. But most Americans are not aware of it. Some people carry deep feelings of grievance but are unable to talk about them constructively. Unarticulated anger over historic and contemporary injustice leads to a kind of acting out—unconsciously motivated behavior.

These underlying problems won't be resolved until we get consensus on what to do about social injustice. And to complicate things further, many upwardly mobile Yammies and Old Boys are themselves descended from Europe's peasants and downtrodden, and they also resent their group's treatment at the hands of political, social, religious, and economic elites. Their relative status is threatened by your acceleration. So they, too, feel annoyed at displacement. And they feel injustice and entitlement, based on class and ethnic rivalries. You'll need luck to succeed in such a complex emotional and political environment.

Face Three Cold Hard Truths

We need to face harsh realities. *The first cold hard truth* is that you are going to be seen as having divided loyalties. You want social and organizational changes. And that's a threat.

The second cold hard truth is that African Americans generally have not established a comparative advantage or a strong performance reputation in any business specialty or in any industry. You won't be a candidate for senior line or staff positions until black people generally are perceived as competent and reliable. African Americans have to score objective triumphs in management, engineering, law, medicine, the sciences, and investment and entrepreneurship to establish group credibility and self-confidence.

White managers don't fear that black managers will take their talent, knowledge, and contacts and go off and start competing businesses that will capture significant market share. Until black managers generally are able to do that—"if we don't use them here, they'll go across the street and hurt us"—you won't be seen as a truly credible potential contributor to your own company.

It will take a while longer for this stringent condition to be met. Until it is, black managers will frequently be plateaued. Individuals will make it to senior levels in congenial situations, usually in Vanguard companies. But in most cases you won't get that opportunity until you are seen as someone who would be a true potential business threat if you were on somebody else's team.

This is yet another reason why black businesses that break through and become major players in mainstream markets will, as a secondary benefit, provide the leverage black managers in traditional major corporations need to assert their own claims to senior management. Until that happens, your bosses will feel they can get along fine without you.

Given current growth, five to ten Black Enterprise 100 companies will probably overlap the Fortune 1000 in the next ten to twenty years. As these competitors show muscle and take market share, you'll see true respect and opportunities open up in the Fortune 1000. But until then, you'll continue to face the kind of ambivalent, resistant, half-hearted associations you now encounter.

Cold hard truth number three is that you have an instant credibility problem with *some* people in *any* setting, because of their preconceptions about black people. Especially if you're in an Old Guard company, you probably would not be in the job you are in, or in any one comparable, if your bosses had their druthers.

Be Realistic but Optimistic

Even after you face these cold hard truths, be optimistic. You can effectively lead, manage, have a satisfying career, and do it all in a way that comports with your deepest values. We think there will be an African-American CEO of a Fortune 500 company by the year 2000. She or he will be an extraordinary Blue Chip.

Sometimes you may feel underutilized and undervalued. And you'll meet Old Boys and Yammies who have reservations about your technical competence, business sense, and decisiveness, even though they may be the ones about whom there should be doubts. Trust yourself.

Mode 1

Joe Wilson, 51, is one of the pioneering high-ranking black line managers in a major manufacturing company.

"Yes, I've faced racism. But the way to deal with a bad situation is to get out if you think a problem is racial. You can't prove it. So go where you'll be comfortable. But do it nicely. You can't scream, 'He's a racist.' That will hurt you, because nobody likes a tattler. Finesse it, or people will think, 'The first time I do something he doesn't like, he'll scream, "Racist." ' "

Jack Davidson, 40, is an international consultant, and a lawyer, with an MBA.

"Blacks who do well in first-line management consulting have been strong, assertive, and quick. But clients only have limited tolerance for those qualities in black professionals. So you need extra skills and balance.

"My problem had little to do with race. The firm had strong views on how people should look and behave. Blacks often didn't fit. Our main competitor, on the other hand, is more flexible with people who don't quite fit. They say, 'What's this guy good at? How can we use him to the max with clients where he can function and contribute?' More companies should think that way.

"We complain about old-boy networks and unfair favoritism. But the game always will be who you know. Hiring is based on knowing people you trust. That's logical and human. You have to reduce psychological risks. That's why you need endorsements and recommendations."

Mode 2

Adele Belmont, 45, grew up in the Midwest, went to New York, where she worked in publishing. After law school, she settled into real estate finance.

"People see my personal characteristics and competence more than demographics. I don't recall any overt discrimination. But I'm sure it happens constantly and subtly."

Ben Allison, 44, is a political scientist, a former academic, and now a planner in a computer company.

"Of course, whites have lower standards to meet than blacks. We're overly scrutinized and challenged. Whites can propose ideas, barely think them through, and get them accepted. But we have to be more thorough."

Mode 3

Andy Rankin, 50, has worked in the private and public sectors as a consultant and policy analyst.

"My boss had gone out of his way to hire me, a first in his division. But three years later, I felt underpaid. No response. So I got angry. He said, 'You sure look out for number one.' Would he have said that to one of my colleagues, asking for a raise commensurate with training, experience, and performance? Maybe I went about it wrong. Not tactful, and bad timing.

"Then, I went into a bank at assistant vice president, because a black vice president pushed for me. One guy in my department almost mutinied. He said, 'I resent that you came in at AVP when it took me years to get AVP.'

"Later, I managed two senior analysts, Al and Bill. They both had wanted my job. Al was insubordinate. Bill was backstabbing. But I established a decent relationship with Al. I'd go to his office and talk about work, life, and listen to his concerns. So, after a rocky start, it was okay.

"I wasn't authoritarian. I was collegial. I respected them. The problem was to get beyond initial reactions. They assumed I would be autocratic and give orders. But that's not my style. Folks react before you have a chance to show what you're about."

Ted Weaver, 52, is a headhunter and former personnel manager in the airlines industry.

"Racism's bad, but I've also worked for white clients who personally went on the line and bucked prevailing sentiment to bring in blacks. In some cases, they later got screwed by their bosses for doing that. And we need to appreciate that."

Arlene Nash, 40, is in information systems in a federal agency.

"No question, whites assume blacks aren't as facile, sophisticated, knowledgeable, but are raw energy and supersensitive, defensive, looking for slights. Whites presume they're normal and blacks aren't. I'm seen as arrogant, and people don't mess with me. So personal style, bearing, and demeanor are important weapons. I'm sure I used to drive my boss crazy. But he didn't show it."

3

Starting Out on the Right Foot

"Concentration is my motto—first honesty, then industry, then concentration."

Andrew Carnegie

"The readiest and surest way to get rid of censure is to be correct ourselves."

Demosthenes

"Get on the good foot."

James Brown

You have almost an equal opportunity, almost everywhere, to be hired at entry level. And you can move up in many companies. There are still impediments and ceilings, glass and otherwise. But before you worry about them, get off to a good start.

What's the key to a surefooted career start? In the first few years:

- Get good training.
- Develop a specialty and confidence in it.
- Find three role models to emulate.

- Add value to some projects in a way that bears your personal stamp.

Along the way you are certain to make mistakes. But don't worry. Just study them and draw careful lessons. Become a student of the art of management. That will, over time, minimize trial and error.

In the early 1980s, the business press started wondering how to rekindle corporate loyalty and concluded we'd be better off with less looking out for number one. In the 1990s, we were hearing more of that theme. But you *do* have to look out for yourself, even in Vanguard companies noted for management development and fairness.

There's also wide concern about management quality. Journalists and academics probe how the way Americans manage—and mismanage—affects overall economic performance, especially compared to our primary world competitors. But we should want to be excellent managers for the job's own sake—for the inherent beauty of an art well practiced—not just because our competitors are eating our lunch.

In the 1960s and 1970s, American managers were concerned with racially integrating entry and lower management. Now, you have skills many companies need. Recruitment and initial development are no longer the heavy focus of affirmative action. Now, it's a question of quality staffing. It's not what the company can do for you but what you can do, unhindered, to help your company.

The problem is that many Old Guard businesses haven't recognized or admitted that part of the solution to their business problems lies in using your abilities fully. Many still think you are somehow part of the problem rather than part of the solution.

Preaching, marching, complaining, and suing won't change that. Only seeing competitor Vanguard companies, with talented black managers, taking away market share and outperforming those who exclude or waste talent will. It's a bottom-line test. Either you make a positive, value-added difference, or you don't. Put up or shut up is the attitude you'll often encounter. Let's see what you've got.

What You Can Do

These lessons apply early in starting a career. And they are useful at every stage in Vanguard and Old Guard companies, especially when you go to new assignments or take laterals or promotions.

Figure Out Your Boss's Strengths and Weaknesses

Observe your superiors, and especially treat early jobs as case studies in management. Pay special attention to your immediate boss. Whatever your boss's weaknesses, he has strengths, things he likes to do, and things he does well. He has a comparative advantage in *something*. Figure out what that is—you might even ask him—and focus on it. Take the initiative and talk to him.

Discover what's important to him. And try to accommodate. Never mind what you think he should do instead, or whether he emphasizes the wrong things. You can't do anything about that. And it won't help to criticize. If you're in an Old Guard company, the fact that you're young, black, and perhaps better formally educated, with more up-to-date analytical tools, will heighten his insecurities.

Concentrate on your boss's priorities. Work to his strengths. Learn something from every assignment. Even if your talents are not fully used, or your accomplishments not fully appreciated, accent the positive, work steady, find a niche, and focus.

Ask yourself:

- Does she *listen well?* Can you talk about problems, ideas, or your ambitions without threatening her?
- Is she a *teacher and coach?* If so, take advantage and learn.
- Is she a *role model?* If so, emulate her approach.

If you're in a Vanguard firm, you're fortunate. In too many companies, too many managers—black and white—are poorly prepared. Cronyism, favoritism, seniority, and racism account for their being managers in the first place. In such companies, dealing with defective managers may be as much of a problem for you as race relations. Indeed, race relations suffer, in part, because too many managers are inadequate. These poor managers' mistakes account for much waste and ineffectiveness. Add incompetence to racism, and the situation gets even dicier.[2]

Face the Bad News

The more your style, values, politics, and savvy fit the cultural norm in your firm and industry, the better—no matter what kind of boss you have. But most African-American managers, including you, don't have optimum characteristics either. They're flawed or inadequate, too. So the juxtaposition of flaws creates problems. How do yours match theirs? What's the mismatch? What's the solution?

One answer is to correct your flaws. That's your primary task, as you start and throughout your career. Don't bother criticizing their faults. Old Guard managers who are defective lack perception, vision, awareness, and sensitivity. They have hierarchical, mechanistic assumptions. They use fear and formal power as management tools, are obsessive and compulsive about petty procedures, authoritarian, controlling, and insecure, and can't lead, inspire, establish trust, or earn respect.

As we said, most managers have a strong point or wouldn't have survived. But the Peter Principle operates: managers tend to be promoted to the level at which they are over their heads—their level of incompetence.

That's the bad news. In too many companies, the boss lacks skill in working with talented, independent-minded, autonomous, self-respecting people. Add race and look out! Unless you're in a Vanguard company, an elite industry leader, chances are your boss will be uncomfortable with a mutually respectful professional relationship with you.

American managers are usually accomplished technical specialists. They can conceive, design, research, produce, finance, and market widgets or services so they are doing something right. But their organizing teaching, coaching, communicating, and "people skills" are too often deficient. So figure out your boss's deficiencies. And look out for how they affect you.

Most managers underdevelop and undervalue "human resource management," believing it soft and trivial. Or they think they're naturally skilled and need no training. So look out for lopsided managers—technically sound but deficient as leaders, or vice versa.

If you're in an Old Guard company, you have a 75 percent probability of having a weak, defective boss at some time in your early career. After that, your chance of having better managers improves because sounder people tend to move ahead.

Too many managers focus on process rather than results. They live by standard operating procedures (SOPs) rather than by independent, professional judgment. They lack vision. In traditional, Old Guard cultures and in industries that are growing slowly or not at all—industries like transportation, insurance, natural resources, utilities, defense, and banking, for example—seniority, favoritism, and cronyism play a large role and produce such bosses. But in Vanguard growth companies and industry leaders, chances are your boss will be fully competent.

Understand Status Incongruence

There is also the problem of status and style mismatch. When you and your boss don't match on professional, social, and demographic levels, that's incongruence. Your organization is socially complex and, therefore, risky. Status incongruence produces strains, insecurities, misjudgments, misunderstandings, slights, and conflicts. That's also bad news. But most managers in Old Guard companies don't fully recognize how their style or even personality affects others. Many racial conflicts can be traced to managers' failure to take account of staff mismatches in age, gender, background, ethnicity, race, and professional standing. They put round pegs in square holes and then wonder why there is strife.

Set High Standards for Yourself

Don't be satisfied just to get along or get by. At the beginning of each rating period, find out what it will take to get a 10 or an

A. To get the most out of each job, do more than expected. Satisfy your boss's expectations, then go beyond that and satisfy your own. The payoff comes when your experience, skill, and accomplishments land you in a choice spot. Become good enough so you can go work for a competitor and help it outperform your current company. Until senior managers perceive that as likely, you won't be as highly regarded as you hope.

Make Friends With the Solids

Identify Solids. (We met them in chapter 2.) Get to know them. They'll stand you in good stead when things are tough. Find a way to support them and contribute to their success, directly or indirectly. Build relationships based on trust, reciprocal professional respect, shared values, and personal and social compatibility.

Hit the Ground Running

You may feel you have a grace period to get up to speed. Don't bet on it. Other people may, but you're being watched and judged from day one, even if your boss says you can ease into it.

Be Prepared

Your boss will be pleased that you come to meetings having defined problems clearly, thought through them, and done your research, and you'll get more challenging assignments from people who notice and appreciate your ability.

Too many meetings are poorly run and waste time. Least-common-denominator solutions are chosen because problems are poorly defined. Meetings waste time and produce little because of group dynamics and politics and also because preparation is lacking. That's often the reason for poor decisions and poor results.

Don't Let Anyone Intimidate You Intellectually

Know what you're talking about and what you're doing. Become an expert. Build strong analytical skills.

Stanford University psychologist Harold Leavitt says that skilled analytic types enjoy high status. They appear superior to less effective analysts. And they tend to play games. They see you as an opponent and try to one-up you. They emphasize method over content. This behavior is actually about power. And since you're often assumed to be less quantitative, some colleagues will try to dominate you by intimidating you with numerical virtuosity.

They will use a pseudoanalytic style to assert superiority. They use hard analysis and quantitative overkill as a game to set up informal hierarchies among people who are formally peers. But these analytical games have little to do with defining or solving problems. So watch for this game.

Establish Your Specialty

Organizational politics, social connections, and good sponsorship are important. So is luck. But for you, technical competence is most important. It determines how you take off and how far you go. Work on your specialty and build confidence and mastery.

Take Responsibility for Your Own Development

Companies like Wells Fargo, Proctor and Gamble, Citibank, GE, and IBM offer high-quality training. Classroom and programmed assignments build skills and confidence. Graduates are highly marketable. You're groomed, get your ticket punched, and move along. You have an equal opportunity to enter and move up for fifteen years or so. Then you'll notice the ceiling. But at the outset, you have a fair chance.

Many young managers think the human resources, personnel, or training departments will make the right rotation available at the right time. But *you* are in charge of that, not they.

Even the best Vanguard companies misuse some talent, black and white. And Old Guard companies often mess up young careers. You can be undertrained, underchallenged, underutilized, and arrive at your fortieth birthday wondering why your marketability suffers because of gaps in experience or lack of sub-stantive achievements in the resumé you thought looked pretty good.

Don't count on employers to design your career. Sloppy train-ing and development is common. But you have to be more vigi-lant than others. Your bosses are ambivalent. They want you on the team and off at the same time. That's doublethink. So don't be complacent, even in a Vanguard company.

Seek assignments, look for challenges, nominate yourself for training, and network with Solids who will tell you about oppor-tunities. Don't wait for your boss or the personnel department to invite you.

Volunteer for Special Projects

If your company is enlightened, you are capable, and your boss wants you to contribute, challenging assignments will flow *to* you. But in many places, your presence causes anxiety, and your talents are doubted or are a threat. So find projects that stretch you. Take the initiative, offer your services, do extra work, and be visible. Try for projects that produce a report that bears your name as part of the team so your contribution lives on.

Because you're visible, your boss may ask you to get involved in projects outside your scope of work. These can keep you from concentrating on mastering technical skills and developing deep expertise. She may ask you to sit on committees on issues not directly your concern because she wants a black perspective or representative. If your input gets serious attention, that can be an advantage, but it can also waste time. So be selective. Don't become window dressing. Make sure that the assignment is gen-uine and important to your boss and that she takes account of it when rewarding and evaluating you.

Know your role on the team. Be clear about what's expected. Don't let it be ambiguous. At annual goal-setting time, think through how these special assignments fit your overall role and progress.

Living With Stereotypes

Most Old Boys and Yammies who have never worked with an African-American peer have stereotyped ways of thinking about you. If they resist your suggestions, conclusions, or initiatives, they may be motivated less by personal hostility than by unfounded assumptions about your competence. But do these affect how they work with you? Does this complicate your life, distract you, diminish your achievements? That's your concern, not the mere stereotyping.

What can you do about stereotypes? They may have some basis, so first make sure they don't apply to you. Don't try to show "you're not that way." Just do your best work. Achieve your goals. And remember, you're a walking contradiction. They're afraid you'll do well, and also that you'll do poorly. But that's their problem. Keep your eye on the achievement prize.

Write Well

How well you do, how colleagues and staff respond to your ideas, has a lot to do with how you write. So take night courses if necessary and practice. Read books on writing. Think about it. Most managers don't.

One reason so many business units underachieve and function poorly is that their manuals, SOPs, regulations, and directives are badly written. They reflect poor thinking. They're redundant, obscure, indirect, passive and bureaucratic. Quality writing affects the company's economic performance. Well-written memos and reports get better results. Make sure your writing is tight, economical, thoughtful, and brief. Don't write like a bureaucrat, even if you work in a bureaucracy.

Race is a factor here, too. Just as some expected you to be weak quantitatively, you may be expected to have trouble with the King's English. After all, one racial stereotype is of nongrammatical English. So if you're merely grammatical, it will surprise many. But go further. Be clear and tight. Write in plain English, something too few managers do. Make your writing influence, persuade, convince, demonstrate, and sell.

Continue Your Education

Your education as a manager should never end. Get in the habit of continuing it now. Take mini courses, short courses, long courses, night and day courses, in house, out of house, off campus, on campus, traditional, innovative, individual self-study, small group, large group, specialized, and general training. Take courses in management, technical subjects, and even art, music, and literature.

Handle Your Money Wisely

Move quickly toward financial independence. From day one, save and invest conservatively. Aim for substantial nonsalary income by age forty.

You'll make mid-career decisions with more confidence if you can look at a tough job situation, and even walk away from a bad scene, without feeling trapped by financial constraints. It's not really a matter of "take this job and shove it," but some black managers are too risk-averse, often because of debt burdens, ill-advised financial commitments, and sour investments that become overwhelming constraints.

Too many young managers conspicuously consume: fancy cars, clothes, gadgets, travel, entertainment. That's a mistake. Even though your income enables you to live in a style you've long dreamed of, your better move is disciplined saving and investment, because your professional freedom and integrity depend on fiscal strength.

Finally, Get Satisfaction Outside the Job

At work, be alert, prepared, diligent, goal-oriented, clear about your role, and persistent in honing your skills. But maintain perspective on where work fits in your life. Have multiple sources of satisfaction. Home and family, athletic, spiritual, cultural, artistic, community, and political interests—start right away to cultivate these and keep them in balance. It's easy to become one-dimensional. Don't let your career overwhelm everything else. Guard against one-sidedness.

Of course to reach senior management, you have to make trade-offs. Work will average seven A.M. to seven P.M., plus Saturdays and Sundays. You'll have to forego other pursuits. There'll be lots of travel and frequent relocations. Most managers discover, at some point, they're not prepared to continue to pay that price, especially since the loyalty is often not repaid.

A well-balanced life is the one for most managers who finally conclude they are not going to become senior executives in any event. The odds are long against making it to a Fortune 1000 executive suite. But you can still take pleasure, on and off the job. Work on your backhand. Write poetry. Swim, run, raft the Colorado, climb in Nepal, garden, do macramé, fingerpaint, sing in the choir, collect antiques, refinish furniture, raise beagles, help at the hospital, advise a scout troop. Start now. Live.

Be moderate in desire. You create problems by wanting too much or too intensely. This doesn't mean you should be satisfied with pittances. But your appetites can be insatiable. So don't count on reaching objectives by political manipulation.

Former California Governor Jerry Brown kept a Latin inscription in his office: *Age Quod Agis*. Do What You Are Doing. Concentrate on the task. He also was consciously spiritual at work. This doesn't mean overt spirituality or religiosity.

But there's a spiritual dimension to many successful managers. If your view of life includes a spiritual element, feel free to apply it to your job. If you believe that prayer helps solve problems, pray. If you believe that the Golden Rule or some other ethical tenet is a key to human relationships, employ it consciously. If you believe that transcendent values—intuition, higher consciousness, the Great Spirit, or God—should guide your decisions, feel comfortable with your inner-directed orientation toward managing If you believe that the hype about making it, competition, toughness, and looking out for number one is bogus, empty, and meaningless, live according to your different drummer.

It you find that management values stressing cooperation, participation, trust, intrinsic meaning, sharing, openness, and support for others have greater worth, live accordingly. Spiritually conscious, soulful management will gain adherents and will prove well tuned to organizations' needs. But even if you feel ahead of the curve, out of step, odd, or nonconformist because your style reflects these values, and even if you believe it opens you up to penalties, be true to the core of your spirituality.

The Modes and How They View Early Career Strategy

Mode 1 managers believe it's important not to rock the boat. Make the boss's priorities yours, no matter what. Adopt the company point of view and learn to fit in. You aren't there to change anything. Just do the job. Find out how the game is played and play it.

Mode 2 managers believe it's okay to question policy and practice. But the key is scoping out a career strategy that maximizes returns at each level and leverages them into gains at the next. Develop your own training strategy and look for good projects and assignments. Concentrate most of all on building technical self-confidence and strong reputation.

Mode 3 managers concentrate on growth—learning and building your own human and financial capital. But they don't compromise values to ingratiate themselves, because integrity, political or otherwise, is their overriding concern. Unfortunately for Mode 3s, they get into conflicts more often than the other modes and are often seen as having an "attitude."

Mode 1

Stu Elmore, 50, worked in investment banking on Wall Street, ran a government regulatory agency and is a successful investor and consultant.

"The issue is not skills, it's attitude. It's not where you went to school or how smart you are but: Are you on my team. Can I trust you?

"Personality is key. Winning and leadership are done through personal qualities. Especially in selling. That's most important. But establish a humility level, even though you have a big ego. And another thing—from the beginning, save and invest prudently. Conserve cash. That gives you freedom.

"Most white folks come in the room challenging everything you say because they believe their stuff is good—better than yours. They believe that even when they're right out of school, no matter how much more experience you have.

Mode 2

Joe Wilson

"To get a good start, get good in your specialty. Keep your head down for the first eighteen months. Do what you're asked. You're being tested. You might want to say, 'That's not what I went to school for. That's too mundane.' Do it anyway. Show you're a team player."

Linda Jackson, 40, is an MBA in a senior financial position in a major communications company.

"I was good at finance. But you can become too specialized. If you want to be a general manager, you need breadth. But I want to eventually own my own company. So moving to the top here wasn't my objective."

"But it's a drawback not having sales and production experience. They're not critical. People who run companies without broad experience do all right. But for black people, it's good to have breadth so folks won't have that excuse. 'You don't have this experience. You don't have that.' It's an obstacle."

"They promote others with narrow experience. But we need breadth as insurance. It makes you a better executive. But a lot of people have narrow backgrounds, move into general management, and do well.

"If I'd had better bosses early on, it would have led to more varied experience, and I'd be better off. Be assertive. Some companies, like IBM, have structured development. They're paternalistic. But in others, you have to make your own way. Not too many people are happy with the way they've been developed."

Stan Mangam, 38, is a manager in electrical equipment.

"Mistakes don't mean inferiority. Don't lose confidence after a mistake. Black managers get down on themselves too hard. That hurts performance."

Mode 3

Ben Pringle, 48, is a consultant and entrepreneur who worked internationally in marketing.

"If I wanted a position, I lobbied directly for it. I said, 'Watch me.' I'd do my job well, then go back and ask, 'Do I get the job?' I'd sell myself. But the school solution might be more subtle. Not as direct. More social schmoozing."

Andy Rankin

"I've had bosses that were bureaucrats who survived on guile. But I'd get clear on objectives, know what they wanted accomplished, then do it. My first firm didn't have a development program. My boss was laid back. So I wasn't challenged. If there isn't good training and rotation, push for assignments. Create your own developmental program."

Brad Graham, 42, has worked in marketing for a multinational company and with a major defense contractor.

"I started in New York in consumer products. Park Avenue. Feeling pretty good. My product manager wanted a relationship outside of work. But I thought, 'They don't really want me here.' I wanted to be comfortable. But they wanted me to make *them* comfortable, to be like them.

"I wanted to keep my personal and professional life separate and to hold onto my 'blackness.' The other two black MBAs' demeanor made them comfortable. But I was seen as an arrogant Harvard MBA. I wasn't abrasive. I had good interpersonal skills. But if I had a strong view, I'd say so. I didn't endear myself. I should have socialized more. We had drinks after work, but that was it.

"An older black gentleman came around every day to shine shoes. The first time he saw me, he seemed puzzled. But I didn't want him to shine my shoes. He could have been my grandfather. He joked with the whites, and they'd laugh. But that turned me off. It was a reminder that things weren't as they should be.

"If I were doing it over, I would socialize more and get to know them better. But longer term I wouldn't have been in contention for general manager or group product manager anyway.

"There was a style problem. My boss tried to tell me how to arrange my office, my bookcase, my desk. But I kept it the way I wanted it. I took it as, 'They're trying to remake me into something I'm not.' So I battled, made my little statement. But ultimately, I lost. Everyone has a sense of what's fair and right. If someone is petty, rather than see the big picture, I fight. So, inevitably, I wasn't going to hit it off with this guy."

4

Making the Most
of Performance Appraisals

"All men are great, in their dreams."

SIGMUND FREUD

"In the eyes of the people, the general who wins a battle has
made no mistakes."

VOLTAIRE

"Life ain't been no crystal stair."

LANGSTON HUGHES

Become knowledgeable about appraisal. Learn to do it well by
taking extra courses, like the American Management Association's.
And actively participate. Don't simply go along passively with the
annual process.

The story goes that Henry Ford II fired Lee Iacocca by simply
saying, "I just don't like you very much." This version of events
may be apocryphal, or at least incomplete. But personal bias *is* a
factor in many evaluations. Especially in Old Guard companies,
appraisal isn't merely about objective assessment of performance.
If you don't prevent it, it becomes heavily subjective and weighted

by whim based on social factors and chemistry. Personal likes and dislikes will probably not be made explicit and put on the record, but they are often a major factor in appraisal.

You, more than most Yammies and Old Boys, need to be knowledgeable about how to do appraisal right. Suppose, at your next evaluation, your boss says some aspect of your work is unsatisfactory. How would you react if you disagreed and thought the weight of the evidence was on your side? In some circumstances, you might even talk to a lawyer—there's growing willingness to assert and defend legal rights. But you'd have lots of company in receiving grossly subjective evaluations.

What You Can Do

Watch for Bias

In the 1980s, Laras Eason, an engineer, sued his employer, General Motors, in a class action suit seeking $100 million in damages. He said the company's evaluation and promotion systems were racially biased. Specifically, he believed white managers tended to evaluate black nonmanagement workers in the middle range of the rating scale, so they received few promotions and merit raises, which made them more vulnerable to layoffs. He also believed white managers used the same tactic to help keep black managers from reaching top jobs—and if black managers complained, GM found ways to discharge them.

It's not likely that GM actually had a formal policy encouraging this. And allegations may be exaggerated. But there's little doubt racial bias influences performance appraisal in most corporations.

If racist bias is affecting your evaluations, it will only show up in *your* sense that a double standard is operating: you know your work is on a par with or superior to your white colleagues', yet you get lower evaluations. Don't worry about it. Move your level of effort up a notch or two, work smarter, and take the lower appraisal as a signal that it's time to move on.

Don't argue that your boss is a racist or that the review reflects racism. What's the point? Your boss knows it, if it's true. And if it's not, what have you accomplished? You create a pointless no-win controversy. Formal appeals and grievances can get a racist on the record, if you can show disparate treatment. But it won't change the way you're viewed.

If managers evaluate on level of activity, not quality or results, your chances of consistently fair, meaningful evaluations aren't high, unless you're in a function with a clear bottom-line impact or in a well-run Vanguard company.

Pepsico is an example of a high-risk, high-reward Vanguard company that stepped back to rethink performance evaluation. It decided people didn't know clearly where they stood, and that was causing alienation. Pepsico now constructively uses reviews to look closely at performance and to clarify what's expected and what will be rewarded. That will also reduce racial bias.

Solids will help you if you need endorsements to counter a negative appraisal. A sound relationship with Solids is insurance against Old Boys' and Yammies' evaluation biases. Solids will offer to put a commendation in your file or to vouch for a project well done. You may sometimes need to seek out position reviews to nullify or modify an unfair negative appraisal.

Not fitting the company image is another basis for bias. If your work is technically solid, and if you're productive and show results that meet objectives, but you don't fit in, you'll be downgraded in subjective appraisal. If your boss is uncomfortable with you, no matter how good your work, you won't get the same scores as someone who reminds him of himself. So be clear about objectives at the outset, then do an outstanding job on the quantifiables.

Understand the Limitations
of the Appraisal Process

Vanguard companies link performance evaluation to contribution to the larger corporate objective, which is often defined as "enhance shareholder value." But it's tough to measure mid-level contributions to that ultimate objective. There are proxy measures—sales, cost reduction, management of resources—but they're all indirect.

Regardless of race, it's hard for most managers in Old Guard companies to know exactly how well they're contributing. Most get inconsistent feedback. Vanguard companies make it a point to have systems that let managers know where they stand, how they're doing, and what things are mutually agreed on.

Most managers are nervous about giving useful evaluations, because it's an awkward situation and because they've not been trained. So they develop rituals to get through the required meeting instead of using it constructively. Too many organizations let them get away with this.

Race increases the discomfort level, so expect your work to be seen through biased filters. These introduce inaccuracies that keep you from learning where you stand, how you're perceived, and how your contributions are really measured.

Of course, one reason candid discussion of performance is avoided is fear of complaints, liable and defamation suits, and discrimination charges under Title VII of the 1964 Civil Rights Act. This fear may restrict your feedback, and that doesn't help you improve performance. So make sure your boss knows you intend to use the process constructively.

Looking ahead, this concern about legal repercussions can limit your company's willingness to give references when you want to move on. Lawyers and personnel staff are often cautious and tell managers to give only dates of employment and little or no other on-the-record information.

Participate in Setting Objectives

Management by Objectives is now a widely used technique, and it may help you get more honest appraisals. The more objective the standard, the more likely you'll get unbiased feedback and performance reviews. The key is, participate fully and creatively in setting your objectives. That's more likely to produce positive results, in your work and in your next appraisal, than having objectives handed to you or, at the other extreme, having your boss just say, "Do your best."

Use the Appraisal Process to Develop

Talk about performance, including the feedback process, with your boss. Initiate such informal sessions frequently—annually or twice a year isn't enough. Your boss may fear confrontation or be poorly trained. So ask for honest, straight opinions in detail so you can use them. Generalities won't do.

You are responsible for knowing where you stand, not your supervisor or the human resources department. Old Boys and Yammies are ambivalent about your performance. They want you to do well, but not too well. So you, more than most, need to use appraisal constructively. To learn more, you can read *Personnel*, *Personnel Journal*, and *Human Resources Management*—these magazines keep you up on new thinking.

And always remind yourself that you don't have job security. Managers used to assume good performance and loyalty earned them security. But no more. Mass layoffs of managers and professionals occur in all industries. Few companies have "no layoff" policies anymore. This heightens insecurity and competition, mistrust and noncooperation. And it leads to tougher and sometimes more biased evaluations. The pressure is on to be lean and clean and profitable. So your margin for error and opportunity to learn from mistakes are restricted even more.

In appraisal, discuss intangibles like style, values, and assumptions about management and leadership. Exchange ideas. Demystify your evaluations. Ask what will it take to get an outstanding rating. Make clear you're not just looking for an acceptable rating—you want to know what objectively has to be accomplished to get the highest rating.

Talk about things you've noticed but about which you've kept quiet. Tell your boss in advance that you intend to raise these issues. "Sally, next month at performance review, I want to get away from the format. Let's talk about management style, values, and how we can really work together."

Make quarterly, annual, and informal reviews opportunities to talk cooperatively. Don't attack and defend. *Critique*, not *criticism*, is what you want. Together, check performance against the negotiated objectives.

Make clear that you want guidance, including wanting to know how you are seen by third parties who talk to your boss.

Say you want appraisals for development. Emphasize this as often as necessary to convince your boss you'll use the sessions constructively and can take bad news. If you're credible and not threatening, you can improve your performance. Once you establish an honest relationship, make sure your boss sees you making changes.

Go in with a game plan, not a seat-of-the-pants approach. Go with your accomplishments written down and emphasize results that fit his priorities. If he recognizes, uses, and rewards talent, you'll benefit.

Evaluate Yourself Critically

Be tough appraising yourself. Be intellectually honest. Face up to your weaknesses and defects. Don't excuse them. Be realistic about your performance. Take a cold hard look at your real, not imagined, contribution. Be your own sharpest critic.

Then your appraisal by others will be constructive. You won't be surprised by anything negative. You won't become defensive about criticism when you know you deserve it. But if you haven't frankly evaluated your own work, you may unexpectedly get negative feedback and erroneously ascribe it to racism.

The Modes and How They Think
About Appraisal

Mode 1 managers say appraisal is basically subjective but fair. There's not much of a problem. And to the extent evaluation is distorted, race plays little or no part. It's other factors that produce poor results. And, in any case, black managers who are low-rated earned it and should focus individually on improving performance and not complain about biased appraisal. The solution is to concentrate on doing what your boss wants; if you consistently satisfy that requirement, you'll grade out high. Don't worry about technical flaws in the process. It's the same for everyone.

Mode 2 managers say the process is flawed and defective but also believe black managers make excessive complaints. Race adds to appraisal distortions. And sometimes the problem is simply poor-quality appraisal, not that appraisal is misused. But black managers should make it a point to be well informed on appraisal technique so they can defend themselves and get maximum benefit from the process. And they should look for irregularities and respond informally to get them corrected.

Mode 3 managers believe the process is often venal and that when it is, it should be resisted and confronted. They look at evaluations with a jaundiced eye and say the system is too often racially biased. Black managers should be prepared to respond formally with individual EEO complaints and legal actions as well as collectively through organizations of black managers like the National Black MBA Association and other industry and professional groups.

Mode 1

Ossie Gordon, 56, an entrepreneur, was a partner in a Big Six firm.

"Our managers got training on giving and receiving constructive criticism. It wasn't better or worse for me than for others. But most blacks feel appraisal hurts them more than whites."

Joe Wilson

"Get a good feel for how they perceive you. Don't get angry at what they say. If you don't like it and you show it, they won't say any more, but it won't change their perception. If there's a racial bias, leave. But lots of managers have racial bias without its affecting their evaluations. Just do a good job and listen to what they think.

"Once, my boss said I'd plagiarized a report. Of course, I hadn't. So I had to leave that situation.

"Things are more competitive today. Companies will drop you like a hot potato even if you've been there forty-five years. Most businesses are now mature. Relentless cost reductions will be a way of life because we don't have the growth. Life cycles have shortened, and growth industries mature quicker. So there are fewer havens and sinecures. We just got rid of a thousand years of service in forty salespeople. You have to perform, and they have to know you're performing."

Walt Thomas, 39, handles financial management in health services management.

"Appraisal has to be ongoing, When it's once a year, it's really about raises, and it's not effective as a development tool. Ideally, you get day-to-day constructive feedback. But I've never been treated unfairly."

Mode 2

Gene Mason, 40, is with a Big Six accounting firm.

"It's damned difficult to win. Performance is key. They look at quantitative results very hard in deciding where to move you."

Jim Waters, 39, works in a nonprofit corporation. He's an MBA and an ordained minister.

"I've had no performance evaluation in this organization. I'm busting my behind but getting no formal recognition, and that disturbs me. I've never seen my formal review or signed it. And I'm number two.

"I've never sat with the president to be evaluated. I'm comfortable with how he feels about me, but everyone needs explicit, regular, predictable constructive feedback. I came to clean up morale problems. I respect my boss's judgment of me. He lets me run this office. But he gives a perfunctory review. We have a great relationship. But I'd still prefer a formal review. He must see things about my work I'd like to know. I asked for it my first year, and he said, 'Let's get together on it,' but we haven't."

Bernie Madison, 51, a Ph.D. engineer and a senior Federal manager, has worked on leading-edge space programs in the private sector.

"Performance evaluation is about how you like a person more than about how they really do. In government, it's a joke. In aerospace, there was more logic to it, more integrity. My boss is Asian. In our annual evaluation, we talk about family, investments, everything but the job, really."

Bob York, 48, is a management consultant and former entrepreneur.

"My supervisor is one of the world's worst at appraisal. But race is not the issue. He's not capable of negative feedback. I don't know how he judges me. You come away thinking you can walk on water. But these kinds of appraisals don't help you improve. It's more difficult if you're evaluated on process or input than on results. And if the boss says something was expected, and this is the first you've heard about it, they're setting you up."

Wes Albright, 50, has an MBA and is an electrical engineer with a major computer company, where he runs an important laboratory.

"My performance appraisals are excellent. But lately there's no commensurate salary increase or bonus. But I didn't challenge it."

Louise Gibson, 38, came from Harvard Business School through a large New York bank to be a senior officer in an innovative, fast-growing financial services firm.

"I have constructive in-depth appraisals. My problem was people saying, 'You're doing extremely well. You're on a fast track,' but still holding me back.

"I was brought into consumer marketing. But the route to the top was through branch management. I had superlative appraisals, but I kept hearing, 'You're too smart for line jobs. We don't put female Top Ten MBAs in those jobs.' They never talked about my being black. Gender was emphasized as creating difficulty. They said I had 'stature,' 'poise,' 'class' that aren't typical of people in those line jobs. But they never brought up a black issue.

"And I pushed for bottom-line responsibility. A process shop in credit cards, or running a bunch of lending offices. I was always in a visible role. I helped the bank figure out how to get deposits outside the home region. I helped plan a program that took the bank into new areas. But I wanted to be a business manager! 'We don't want to waste your intelligence in a line job,' they said. I would point to colleagues and say, 'This doesn't compute. What are you talking about?' But the problem was never solved. So I left."

Ken Sopkins, 36, is a manager in a large California bank.

"Evaluations are too often by the grapevine. They're based on others' opinion rather than your boss's firsthand contact.

Mode 3

Stu Elmore

"They don't want you to improve. Most whites at my level get better performance feedback. When I speak to superiors about performance, I don't bring up weaknesses because they would focus on them. If they bring them up, then, okay. And there's an assumption you aren't capable. Then, when you show you are, that's also resented. On the other hand, if you deserve negative comments you may also not get them because your manager may fear confrontation. Direct, honest feedback that could help you may be withheld out of fear."

Art Barlow, 48, held a senior job in a major consulting firm.

"Before I got to VP, I had a boss who only cared if I made money for him. If I did well for him, he paid me. Later, when I became an officer, my boss was a heavy liberal. And my reviews were too great. My raises and bonuses and stock options were higher than average. But even then, I saw racism in the firm generally.

"I saw comments after hiring interviews of black candidates: 'Does he speak English?' 'He dresses like he's still in the City.' And I saw blacks hired from Harvard and Stanford downgraded in performance ratings. People would write, 'Has no skills.' But for comparable whites, struggling, it was, 'Coming slower than anticipated, but has potential.' Well, that's really the same evaluation, couched differently. But the blacks got shunted aside."

Jack Bell, 50, a marketing manager in computers, has a wall of awards and certificates in his office attesting to twenty years in sales and membership in the 100 club.

"This company was found not guilty of racism in a class action suit a few years ago. The company has a grand plan, but people still have biases. With better plans there'd be less room for individual bias. I like sales because, compared with other areas, it's objectively measured. But they can also screw that up when they want to. They say, 'Yeah. You made 100 percent, but everyone else made 125 percent.' That kind of thing. Managers can hurt you. They can manipulate your territories and quotas set at the beginning of the year. They can set whatever hurdles they want.

"My evaluations were fair until I moved into management. Then they became racial. They have this ideal manager in their heads. But no one can be that in a changing environment as competitive and market-driven as this one.

"Even when you concur in the ideal, there are always exceptions that should be taken account of, problems that crop up during the year. But they can play hard ball, and refuse to take account of extenuating circumstances, and focus narrowly on the objectives you didn't fully meet. That's how racial bias gets acted out—by refusal to take account of realities that interfered with reaching some objectives in your case, but not in others.

"Every time I'm evaluated, there's a tough discussion. And it gets histrionic, if not emotional. Blacks have to be paranoid and not trust the system. The old adage—if you're white, you're all right, if you're brown, stick around (meaning in this case Hispanic or Asian), and if you're black, stay back—that's still true. If you're black, whites don't trust you, unless you bend over backwards to prove yourself. But some hoops we're asked to jump through, no self-respecting person with integrity will go for.

"I was a marketing manager in Ohio. One night I went to the airport to take a trip, about ten P.M. And there was the administrative assistant to the regional manager. I said, 'Hi, Bob. Where you off to?' He said, 'I'm just waiting for Harry [the regional manager]. I'm getting his bags and driving him home. And, in the morning, I'll pick him up again.'

"Now, my father was a chauffeur. I wouldn't be able to bring myself to do that for a boss. You know what I'm saying? And other blacks tend not to be able to stoop to do things like that to curry favor with a boss. We don't do apple polishing.

"But white boys do it every day. That's what it takes to get ahead, in many cases. And their peers don't down them for it. Oh, they may kid them about brown-nosing. But that's not the same as being called an Uncle Tom.

"Here, blacks who made it to vice president—and there are several—have been able to bring themselves to do these kinds of things. But that's just too high a price for many of us.

"The company also has subtle rules that bar black advancement. No mustaches, no facial hair or sideburns. A close-cropped haircut. And, most of all, give up your friends, and adopt their friends. See? The barriers are tricky. You can be accepted. You can make friends and join the scene, if you're willing to give up who you are.

"I've seen black managers—who were good—try to do it their own way, to buck that system. But in two or three years they hit the screen and were not on the fast track any longer or were gone. But if you become part of the culture totally, you can get ahead even without outstanding ability. The best talent does not necessarily rise to the top. You have to play the game.

"In evaluation, positive and negative are brought up. But the rating will be in the middle. If they want you to move ahead, if you're favored, they'll give you 1s and 2s. But most of us get 3s and 2s. I got 2s steadily, but after I became a manager, I got my first 3. 'Yeah, Jack. You had a good year, but there were these problems.'

"Your manager gives you a performance plan. It can be too general or too specific. That's another game that allows for bias.

"We also have an open-door policy. If you have a problem with an evaluation, you can go up several levels to see about changing it. You can even ask for a formal investigation. I used that and won the battle but lost the war, because a whispering campaign starts. 'He complained and may be tough to manage.' So it hurts in the long run. The whispered word is a bitch. You can try to neutralize whispers. But the best approach is, to find a good manager and perform so you can fix your reputation.

Rod Clark, 55, is an electrical engineer who owns an electronics company in California. Earlier, he had been in senior management at a large computer company. Then he hit the ceiling and left.

"Some, and perhaps many, businessmen have a Shockley view of our native intelligence and capacity to do well in high tech. They don't respect our basic competence. (Stanford's late professor William Shockley believed blacks are, on average, intellectually, genetically inferior to whites. No doubt some managers in Old Guard technical and basic industries share that opinion. They may grudgingly respect your work yet hold generally racist beliefs and see you as an exception. Their beliefs bias appraisals.")

Brad Graham

"I always know what's expected, and I leave no room for assumptions. But one situation taught me a hard lesson. I've never told anyone but my wife. But I guess I'm old enough to be objective.

"Right after business school, I worked closely with an ad agency. The agency people were more liberal than my colleagues. One day, the agency's account executive took me aside and said, 'You should get out of here. Do you know they're telling jokes about you? Your own colleagues? They're racists.'

"I was called in shortly after that for an unscheduled appraisal. My boss, who was like a buddy, said, 'I won't waste time talking about all the things you do well. I want to go over some issues.' So, far thirty minutes, he told me all the things I was not doing to his satisfaction: working with the ad agency, writing, communicating in general, setting priorities.

"What he described was actually the total job. I was livid. I said, 'What the hell are you doing?' I was being railroaded by this guy I had naively trusted. Next, his boss tells me they want to take a closer look at me. Then I recalled what the ad agency guy said. No warning, no feedback. A negative appraisal. Then they gave me added assignments. I was working way beyond the normal hours everyone else worked. They were loading me up to fail. And not long after, I left."

Earl Newsome, 52, a lawyer in private practice, has held senior government posts.

"I get glowing evaluations about leadership ability, judgment. The narrative would lead you to expect a 1. But the rating would be a 2.

"I have a self-containment that deals with whites' presumptions. And they see I'm not fully committed. If you believe in the company and don't save something for yourself, they feel free to misuse you. So hold something back. But it's a catch-22. Holding back leads to lower performance appraisals.

"Whites have problems with blacks who are equal or better in ability. This creates new appraisal problems. They don't expect that self-assured attitude. They see it as arrogance, and they respond at review time.

"When you're under their control, they've got you, and they can put you down. And you can internalize their negativity if you're not careful. So don't let them define you. Otherwise, you risk underestimating yourself."

5

Working With Your Boss

"I will praise any man that will praise me."

WILLIAM SHAKESPEARE

"Keeping out of mischief now."

FATS WALLER

Does something about African-American culture produce a tendency to hyperindividualism, a need for autonomy, and a resistance to authority and hierarchy? Many black managers thrive and do their most creative and productive work when controls and constraints are minimized—when they can improvise. In a sense, they can be called "the Jazz Managers." That doesn't mean undisciplined, but it does mean unfettered.

If that's true, it's an approach that's slightly ahead of a general trend toward freedom from arbitrary, authoritarian management. That healthy and functional attitude started with Vanguard companies, but it's finding a place even in Old Guard companies. No matter where you work, be conscious of alternative working styles and choose the best response for your situation.

What You Can Do

Size Up Your Boss

First, size up your boss. Determine her motivations and her relationship with her boss, her concerns, her self-image, and how she defines herself. What does she want to maximize? What are her business, personal, and political goals? How does her agenda fit yours? Find two or three of her goals that you especially can support, and concentrate on these.

Find out:

- what she expects from you
- how she sees your subordinates
- what, if anything, went wrong with your predecessors
- what went right
- what she likes best about her own job

In an Old Guard, hierarchical company in a traditional industry, chances are your boss is politically more conservative than you. He's probably ambivalent about you. He may be in over his head—Peter Principled. On the other hand, if he's a Solid, or even a Star—and he's technically knowledgeable, perceptive, sensitive, thoughtful, and analytical, and a talented, aware leader, teacher, and coach—you're in luck. Whatever his strengths or weaknesses, and wherever he is on the racism scales, personal and policy, figure out how to work together to accomplish his priority objectives.

Focus on Mutual Strengths and Interests

Find two or three of your boss's goals that you can especially support. Concentrate on these. If you admire and respect him, working hard to achieve his goals will be no problem. Even if he's an Old Boy, focus on the craft, and communicate, but keep a safe distance so you don't become a target if his fortunes change for the worse.

Questioning his ideas or priorities is dangerous. And it can get you labeled a *Bad Attitude*. You don't need that. So do what he wants first, then do what else you see needs doing.

Avoid Careless Mistakes

Yammies and Old Boys have more room for error and generally are allowed to learn from their mistakes. They feel less pressure to be mistake-free. But you're likely held to a stricter standard, even if it's not spoken. And there's a rational basis for that. In terms of subjective probabilities, your boss feels he has reason to worry that you could make costly mistakes.

He probably believes, based on the cultural consensus, that African Americans, in general, perform at lower levels. So he predicts, based on some combination of objective, subjective, and anecdotal information, that you may, too. In any case, you can be set back in ways your colleagues won't be. Since your bosses have nervous expectations, they may change your assignment, with little or no explanation, at the slightest sign you're having trouble with it. How you respond to unexplained reassignments can affect how your relationship goes. Being able to adapt will help you regain any lost ground.

Clarify Your Role and Your Boss's Expectations of You

To work well with your boss, know what's important to her, and emphasize that. Take care of her priorities first and best. The trouble is, many bosses don't give good guidelines. They think they're clear about what they want, but they often communicate poorly. So get objectives clarified. Ask when you're not certain. Get them spelled out so that you can avoid working on something that's not in the ballpark. Too often, managers just don't know well enough what their boss wants. Your job is to help your boss succeed and to make her look good.

Harvard Business School's D. Quinn Mills sees a changed value system in younger managers. They want to participate in forming strategy, and they care about quality, not just maximizing profit. Older managers, those over forty-five, are more comfortable with strong leadership, hierarchy, clear authority, and exact directives. But "young managers do not see much that is laudable about carrying through a task given them by others. They want to be partners, individuals rather than treated as members of a group."

And young black managers may be even more individualistic. But your need for autonomy conflicts with Old Boys' need for control. Your desire for individual expression and participation is more threatening than a Yammie's, because you are an extra threat to the status quo and implicitly criticize and challenge social, personal, and political assumptions.

Old Boys want you to know your role and your place. If you question assumptions, that's seen as disloyalty. Old Boys feel they must agree with their boss to survive and get ahead. But you're more likely to question and challenge. So the careerist approach may not work for you. And you'd rather not just follow orders. Sometimes you have to go along and swallow your reaction. But despite independent habits of mind, you still have to generally fit in.

Alvin Toffler, author and futurist, says "Third Wave" people protest and fight routine. They want to do valuable work. They mistrust experts and authority. They're self-starters. And they want to participate and help set strategy and direction. If you're a Third Wave person, you threaten traditional authority. And you compound the threat by being black.

Buck Rodgers, an IBM executive, advises managers to:

- Get constant feedback from staff through anonymous surveys.
- Hire people who fit, who are comfortable and compatible with the company value system.

That will maximize the chances that people will understand their boss's expectations. But "fitting in" can be difficult when what's really expected is not just accomplishment but also similar political values, social outlook, habits of mind, and style. Those can be zones of inherent racial differences and conflict with your boss.

Handle Pointless Assignments With Dispatch

What if your boss gives you an assignment you think is a bad idea? If you're in a Vanguard company, where merit determines promotions, and cronyism and favoritism are minimized, you're not likely to get many dumb assignments. But most companies aren't Vanguard, they're Old Guard, and seniority and subjectivity weigh heavily in selecting and placing managers. This creates situations where you can be misused by a marginal boss. If you get a pointless chore, do it quickly and efficiently, then get back to your priority projects.

Anticipate Your Boss's Problems

Pay attention to subtle cues and signals of upcoming trouble. Notice how your boss reacts to organizational changes and to threats and opportunities. Figure out how you can help ahead of time. Offer information and support without being asked. Make yourself indispensable.

Elizabeth Moss Kanter suggests you win favor, support, and rewards by performing above and beyond assignments. Be a self-starter. You *can* do just what you're asked, but it's better to find challenges and opportunities to stretch and grow.

Too often, complaints about being underutilized, isolated, or circumvented reflect the complainer's own lack of energy and imagination. Find opportunities. Don't wait to be invited.

Listen—And See Your Boss's Point of View

An IBM executive heard from a client that "when one of the young white boys comes in, I can talk to him, and think of him as a son, and want to help him. But there's no way I can feel that for a black guy."

That's key. It explains as much as any factor why relations with bosses turn sour or never blossom. Your boss may have trouble identifying with you to the same extent that he does with your white colleagues. Even so, listen to your boss. Look at things from his point of view and give him positive feedback.

Roll With the Punches

That's not easy advice to follow, but it applies to many situations. Let it pass. You can't change your boss's mind unless you're on good personal terms. And race makes persuading even more uphill. You use up goodwill and personal capital when you fuss. So why argue or criticize or complain or explain? It's usually pointless.

Sometimes, of course, you need to have your side of the story or point of view on the record. The more bureaucratic and Old Guard your environment, the more likely this is. In that case, make your case, then let it be. It rarely helps to press an argument.

Arguing, criticizing, and complaining often occur over differences in style more than substance. But expressing differences over style is fruitless. Confronting your boss because you object to how she does things wastes time and alienates.

Disagree Tactfully

Be careful how you point out illogic, shaky assumptions, or wrong but deeply held beliefs. What happens when your analysis or judgment is at odds with his? It's tough for many bosses to hear that from anyone, and tougher from you, especially if you're right. And don't say it if you're not 100 percent sure of your facts and analysis. Don't let your point hurt his self-respect. Stay on the issue. Don't get personal. Messengers often get grief not just for the news itself but for bad timing or delivery. So keep "I told you so," putdowns, or one-upmanship out of it.

Manage your relationship. Develop trust and mutual respect. Remember, your boss catches flak and gets blame and negative feedback from *his* boss. So be positive. He'll appreciate it. The key issue is change. When you find fault or criticize, directly or indirectly, implicitly or explicitly, you threaten and are seen as disloyal in a way Yammies and Old Boys aren't when they do it. When you propose changes or act to cause change, you produce more resistance. You're acceptable if you accept the status quo. But when you seek change, your boss will react. When you say you have a better definition of a problem or a better solution, you may create anxiety.

New ideas threaten. You have ideas and see ways to benefit the company through innovation. But your presence threatens. So how you present ideas is crucial. Package proposals skillfully. Find informal support. Good ideas, on the merits alone, often don't fly. Your presentation has to minimize the threat so your boss will support you.

Avoid Credibility Gaps

What if you give your boss inaccurate facts or analyses that end up causing him embarrassment? You'll have a problem. So be certain about your input. Be careful even in informal discussions. In an Old Guard company, if your judgments prove poor two or three times, your stock will fall fast.

To remain credible and persuasive with superiors, Donald Rumsfeld, former secretary of defense and prominent corporate executive, recommends the following:

- *Be precise.* Imprecise thinking and communicating causes organizational and personal failure.
- *It's easier to get into than out of projects, deals, and programs.* Proceed with caution and check your enthusiasm.
- *Give your boss your best honest judgment.* Challenge conventional wisdom and prevailing notions. And be willing to bring bad news. Don't be a yes-man.

Another set of commonsense rules is:

- *Don't do personal business on company time*, even if others do.
- *Don't boast about achievements.* Just document them and assert them at the right time.
- *Don't be habitually late.* Be early. Stay late. Be first in and last out often.
- *Don't ignore policy or instructions*, especially in an Old Guard company, where process is the focus.
- *Don't whine or complain.*

- *Don't be lazy.* Be a self-starter.

Don't Let the Details Trip You Up

Administrative procedures can be used to trap you. Handling travel arrangements, purchasing, contract administration, inventory and supply issues, using staff services, interaction with clerical and support staffs, office space arrangements, photocopying, the Christmas party, travel vouchers, using the telephone—all the little housekeeping details are areas where a slip-up or a difference of opinion on a minor matter can give a Yammie or Old Boy who is procedure-focused opportunities to attack.

A silly slip can be turned into a federal case, as it were, if he's so inclined. Then you'll waste energy explaining and defending yourself. So, although you may feel administrative details shouldn't take much thought, take care. They can produce little disasters, especially in an Old Guard company where they can be blown out of proportion by anybody who wants to.

Resolve Conflicts

If you're out of sync, and the relationship is deteriorating, it doesn't take much to make it worse. Look at the facts. Perhaps, by omission or commission, you contributed to the problem. Then it's not a trumped-up charge, a matter of misperception, or a simple difference of opinion. If that's the case, admit the mistake. Clear the air. Then move on to the next task. But don't expect to fully recover your standing. When you have made a mistake, taken the initiative, and faced it, you'll still be penalized. Sometimes, of course, you have a valid excuse. If so, state the facts and apologize, then move on.

But you're expected to defer to your boss. Without respect, that's not easy.

Of course, some conflicts aren't based on facts but on values, principles, and different mindsets and worldviews. If you don't fit the culture, don't be a maverick, chronically out of step. Squelch your objections and misgivings, get along with your boss's irrationality and errors in judgment or technique, and avoid this kind of conflict in the first place. That's not easy if you have strong views and are experienced and value autonomy. But to survive, disagree carefully and only on primary matters.

David Ewing's *Do It My Way or You're Fired: Employee Rights and the Changing Role of Management Prerogatives* shows how progressive companies use due process to handle conflict and harassment. Some companies use ombudsmen and counselors to interview and get the truth. But if you're in conflict and think there's an injustice, and use these procedures the racial dimensions may trigger reactions, and right or not, you may lose the war after winning the battle.

So be careful about formal grievances or complaints. In a bureaucracy, you may spend undue energy and capital to win and still come out tarnished. Don't automatically turn the other cheek, but don't press your rights just because you're right. Letting it pass is often the best course. Concentrate on your agenda and long-run strategy.

Don't Ask, If the Answer Might Be No

You have only so much capital, so many chits. When you suggest, propose, recommend, or ask a favor, even just an opportunity, you use scarce capital. Don't waste it on minor matters or ones you haven't thought through. And don't ask, if you think the answer might be no.

Respect the Relationship, If Not the Boss

If you respect your boss, great. The two of you probably have a good relationship. Let him know you admire what he does. Many managers stroke bosses' egos as a tactic. Leave that to others. *Show* respect if you *feel* respect. Praise when it's warranted. Learn from her. Listen actively to her theories of managing and to her aspirations for herself and the unit. Such conversations let you ask how you can help more, and that can only improve your relationship.

But often, bosses are defective, and you'll have a hard time respecting them. Seventy-eight percent of American workers are suspicious of their bosses, say Boston University psychologists Donald Kanter and Philip Mirvis. The most cynical are under twenty-five, less educated, and black.

Listening and supporting won't work without respect. In his book *Coping With Difficult People*, Robert Bronson says even if you don't get along, look for ways to work effectively. Branson types some bosses this way:

- *The Sherman Tank* bullies, yells, interrupts, and puts down subordinates regardless of race. So don't take his attitude toward you as racially motivated or personal. Hold your ground, assert your views forcefully and respectfully, and don't take offense if he attacks.
- *The Clam* is quiet. You have trouble knowing where he stands. So let him know you want to talk, and don't let his silence intimidate.
- *The Complainer* whines and feels victimized. Don't get sucked into whining and feeling victimized along with him. He may also feel threatened, especially if you're a Blue Chip or High Draft. Be direct and businesslike.

There are also other types. In general, listen and perform; that will minimize conflicts with all of them.

- *The Wet Blanket* is a chronic pessimist.
- *The Superagreeable* is an amiable stumbler who unthinkingly interferes in your work.
- *The Indecisive* never gives solid support or clear feedback.
- *The Know-It-All* can never admit you know or thought of something he didn't.

Be Straightforward and Pleasant

Sooner or later you'll be provoked by stupidity and injustice. Your best reaction is to be thoughtful, to express strong feelings, to be straight. Don't play games or communicate indirectly. Say what's on your mind, but as a matter of fact. Report how you feel. Don't blame or attack. Expressing anything negative is risky, even if you're straightforward, candid, and nonthreatening.

Being good-humored doesn't mean shuffle, giggle, scratch, and grin. It means maintain perspective. See the humor in absurd situations. If you get unexpected bad news—you're reassigned, lose a perk, or lose budget—deal with your boss professionally. Don't worry about racial motives. Negotiate to modify the decision, not to win arguments or bring charges.

Remember Your Manners

Common courtesy, good manners, being polite—it all helps. That's common sense. But conflicts often start and fester because of simple lapses in courtesy. Smile. Say "Hello, good morning." Speak when spoken to. Maintain decent if not warm relations with your boss. Injustices that happen will make you angry. But be courteous even when you dislike her for good cause. That's asking a lot, but it's worth the effort.

Take Advantage of Sponsorship

We're led to believe everyone has a sponsor, or mentor. But most people don't. Most managers learn by trial and error. So don't feel sorry for yourself, and don't imagine your competitors have valuable wise support, because they generally face the same situation. And you, like many of them, may have the impression that if you don't have a sponsor, you're in trouble. Not necessarily. Whether you *need* a sponsor depends on your company's culture, your industry, your personal values and strategy, and your personality. You can achieve and enjoy great satisfaction without a sponsor. But for fast promotions—and maximum progress—a sponsor may be important.

Sponsorship should evolve naturally, and the benefits should be reciprocal. Don't *look* for a sponsor. As you follow your course of concentrating on your job and agenda—to develop, achieve, and realize intrinsic satisfaction—a senior manager may discover that you offer sound analysis, consistent sales, reliable judgment, quality production, political support, and other tangible professional and organizational benefits. That's the real basis for sponsorship that will have meaning and value. Altruism, kindheartedness, concern for the underdog, and noblesse oblige are not solid bases for sponsors.

It's tough for interracial sponsoring to work, because implicit trust has to be there, and usually it's not. But some Solids can be excellent sponsors, and the picture is improving. You often hear senior managers don't sponsor people like you because you "aren't like them," and they look for people like themselves. But that's not the point. The point is, you're presumed to want certain changes they don't. If you saw the world as they do, race, per se, would diminish as a barrier to sponsorship. Sponsorship means helping someone prepare to take power, which the sponsor naturally wants that person to use in approved ways. Would you? It's presumed not. That's why it may be hard for you to find one. But it's also why senior black managers should look for talented juniors to sponsor.

The Modes and How They View the Boss

Mode 1 managers accommodate fully, identify with superiors, and submerge most impulses to deviate, disagree, or criticize. They adopt the superior's point of view and agenda with little difficulty or sense of unease or incompatibility.

Mode 2 managers adopt the superior's business agenda but sometimes find that differences in worldview or style create conflicts. They are skillful enough to avoid major set-tos and can work with a wide range of managers despite private doubts.

Mode 3 managers find it difficult to work with people whose views or styles clash with their own or whom they personally dislike. They are critical of and not highly loyal to many superiors and find few who win full confidence and earn professional respect. Therefore, they are frequently out of step with the boss.

Mode 1

Wes Albright

"Despite the troubles and bias, I've respected my bosses. They're good fathers, husbands, community folks. They're human. So don't make broad accusations that demean a person's total character. Make distinctions.

"In industrial companies, you get rewards for long service, not job-hopping. That sustained me, because people at the top have known me fifteen years.

"I've had conflicts with bosses. But if you fight on organizational issues, you get a reputation. I don't get into a fight unless I think I'll win. And nobody wants to hear they're bigots. So saying that about anyone is just not effective."

Ben Pringle

"Talk to your boss. Let him know you're working for him. Produce, of course, but also communicate. Talk to the dude. Make him comfortable.

"My brother was in planning. He let it be known, 'I'd like any job in that new division.' So the division head called him. And my brother gave the 'bottom-line' speech. The division had fifteen salesmen. But many weren't producing. He spotted these and other problems and let the division manager know. In time, he was, in effect, running the division, as his recommendations were adopted. His boss got credit and a promotion. So don't want credit too much. People know who's doing the work. Let your boss take credit. That speaks well for you. Top people know what you did.

"My brother complimented his boss. 'I've learned a lot from you. Now, I'm ready to run a business.' So they gave him one. He cut costs, fixed problems, and made something of it. He increased sales and profits two years running. But it was a dead end. He said, 'I want to be where the action is.' So his former boss, having trouble, invited him back as group vice president. He moved fast, was loyal, did fine work, and didn't step on anybody."

Carl Wilson, 42, recalled his start in the insurance business.

"I developed a natural relationship with the guy who brought me in. He helped me through my divorce, and he taught me the business. He made me stick to it when I got discouraged.

"Try to find a godfather. But a lot of black guys just aren't doing a good job. And nobody'll sponsor somebody not performing. Blacks stop moving up, in part, because there aren't enough seniors to help them. No black executive here has the power to do what my sponsor has.

"It's not kosher in many firms for whites to sponsor blacks. And even at my level, with the help I've had, I was blocked from a better job for no objective reason. But lucky for me, I was able to directly bring up my situation with the CEO, and it quickly got done.

"There's a lot of politics among whites. It's dog eat dog with them. And that affects us and partially determines how we do. Your sponsor's political skill matters. But how good you are is key. It overrides personality, race, and politics."

Mode 2

Jack Bell

"Loyalty is key. Loyalty means, when he's wrong, still back him. Disagree in private, but never go public or escalate. Never embarrass him.

"Get your manager to love you. Do what he asks, and more. Feed his ego without diminishing yourself. Compliment, give credit. Say to others, 'Let me tell you about Jerry. He's one of the best.' And mean it. Of course, sometimes it's bullshit, but it counts. When you score a success, praise your boss. 'I couldn't have done this without him.'

"I criticized management several years ago. Later, my phone was tapped. I was right in my criticism, but I got transferred. After several years of frustration, I claimed discrimination, and lost. You don't claim discrimination here if you have a problem. It's just not smart. What you say is, 'The system didn't work for me.' If you have problems with a boss, don't claim discrimination.

"Bob Henry sued. But the judge said the company was upstanding. And it is. But they ignore individual managers' racism. We train managers on how to behave interracially and be sensitive. One week a year is training in managing people, how to handle marginal employees, super employees, labor relations, etc. We spend big bucks on this.

"The company believes there are four types of people, from very experienced to least experienced. You manage accordingly. You write a management plan for each person each year. You assess each, then guide as needed. The least experienced need lots. The most experienced develop a joint agreement on what they'll do. Then they're more or less on their own. That's enlightened. It respects autonomy. So this company does it well."

Helen Ellis, 38, is a marketing manager in financial services.

"As a technician, I never had conflicts. It was always 'Was it done on time, in budget?' But as a manager, it's 'Was it done right?' And there's more emphasis on personality. Are you someone I'd trust? Do we share interests? Do we enjoy some of the same things? So I've found problems with men. The one woman manager I've had was fine.

"To protect myself, I ally with the boss. Of course, even allies can knife you. So communicate in the open and to the highest level possible. And produce, consistently and predictably. Erratic performance won't fly. But that's not enough. Continually lobby. Let your boss know what you're doing. Keep him informed and on your side. Nothing substitutes for strong informal relationships. That positions you. Warm fuzzies. That's key."

Casey Wrigley, 36, is a district manager for a large insurance company.

"Some black managers make it, but some don't because they're arrogant or lack skills to deal with bosses.

"Here, a black manager hired a white woman. But they conflicted. She goes to her boss's boss, who helps her transfer out. Now, that could be race or personality, but the black manager didn't handle it well. If you're a strong producer, such things wouldn't happen. But he was vulnerable, and his boss didn't mind offending him.

"How good you are makes the difference in personnel and office politics more than personality and race. They look at performance first, at least in bottom-line industries like this, insurance. If your numbers aren't there, you get shunted aside. So some of what happens is our own fault."

Joe Wilson

"Most CEOs of the Top 500 have a personality problem of some kind. My boss, the CEO, and I were having trouble, and he brought in psychologists to work with the two of us. I told them, go talk with the staff first. They did. And sure enough, they came and said I was right. The consensus was, my boss was the conflict's source, not me. If he said he'd do A, I knew he'd do B.

"I started an in-house consulting group. But he hated it, and bad-mouthed it, and had outside consultants have a look. Another time, we gave him a proposal. It would have been awkward to reject it because of the background politics. So he okayed it in the meeting. But I whispered to another guy, 'We will never do this. He'll kill it.' Sure enough, later he took me aside and said, 'We're not doing this. Sink it.' That's how he operated. People outside told me my boss had been hearing the staff preferred to follow me rather than him. They loved me. That set him off, and he turned against me full force from then on.

"Most people don't have problems with race until they're threatened. If you're better, or if you're moving faster, then their true colors come out. So reduce the threat so they won't react like a cornered rat. Probe to see if they're secure. Look for nervous body language. Most people like to talk, so keep listening. You can learn a lot. That's key to getting along with your boss."

Walt Thomas

"In consulting, I was to implement a cost-reporting system for a client. We'd been out in Missouri. At the final presentation, one of the client's managers pulled my team leader aside to talk about me. The next day, back in our offices, a senior VP called me in and said someone had complained I had been stirring up trouble among the client's black employees and had suggested they organize to demand improvements. I said I'd been busy on the case and had done no such thing. Here was someone bothered by my presence, not used to blacks in such situations, telling an outright lie to get me in trouble. I objected strenuously, and my senior VP believed me.

"Sometimes I make a suggestion in a meeting, and it gets no reaction. Then, later, someone else makes the same suggestion, and it's picked up. But it's difficult to conclude it's race. I can be wrong. So I look at my presentation, how and when I make my points, to see if it's adequate.

"Last year, I wanted to participate in union negotiations. I'd made known a year in advance I wanted to be on that team. But I wasn't selected. I had a dual reporting relationship, to regional and to a central headquarters boss. My headquarters boss and I fell out, and I came not to trust her. So she may have kept me off that task force. I think she's as racist as most white people, no more, no less.

"I think of racism as fixed and variable, like costs. Everybody has a fixed, even though low, level of racism, and then a variable component.

"At another agency, working with economists and policy analysts, I worked for months on a project on for-profit hospitals. I gave it to my boss. He said nothing for two weeks. Then he said, 'This isn't quite what I was looking for.' I said, 'Not what you were looking for? I talked to you as I went along. You gave no indication I was on the wrong track. Give me a break. I thought we understood each other.'

"Be more assertive with bosses who play games. Don't put up with b.s. People are competing for fewer jobs. It gets nasty.

Bosses' good intentions and objectivity go out the window. It becomes guerrilla warfare. And it works both ways. To protect yourself in bad relationships with bosses, don't alienate other people. Encourage loyalty and develop a constituency. Be dependable. And do the best job and stay on that."

Ben Allison

"My manager is Hispanic. And he gives me opportunities to talk about anything. He's extraordinary. I work with him very well. I come into business from an academic career with a sense of self based on external sources. But I'm careful not to be labeled by that outside identity. I had to build credibility here and convince them of my value.

"Lots of bosses have no confidence and are afraid that in the crunch, you'll mess up. That's the ultimate key. We've done that more often than we can afford to. Let's admit that, if we're honest. We have to overcome that before we respect ourselves, respect each other, or win respect from bosses. It's not just perception. It's reality. For whatever reasons, there's been too much Amos-and-Andy performance.

"Of course, whites have lower standards for whites than for blacks. We're overly scrutinized and challenged. Whites can propose ideas, barely think them through, and get them accepted. But blacks have to be more thorough.

"Lots of bosses refuse to recognize good work. They'll find something to criticize. That happened to a friend. They were out to get him, and they did. They'd not had a black VP. The Old Boys didn't accept him. He thought like an entrepreneur in a place that's not entrepreneurial.

"They didn't understand his product proposal—thought it was too risky. He was thought of as creative. But he didn't know how to make people comfortable. Didn't stroke them. Stayed to himself. Didn't get to know the people in a position to cut him down. He was brighter than his peers and did good work. But he needed to let them know him personally.

"A headhunter called, once. The company got upset. I took my boss to lunch. I said, 'I'm under pressure. I like it here. What should I do?' He said, 'Do you want a raise?' I said, 'That's not the point. I want advice.' He went back and within three hours arranged a raise. I said, 'That's not what I was after. I just wanted my future clarified. I wasn't out to leverage.' But I was promoted six months later.

"Be careful with those situations. Understand your position. What money do you want? What responsibility? Are you generally satisfied? Don't play games. Don't bite the hand that feeds. Don't trifle with a company that takes care of you. My bonus, two weeks ago, was a signal. So I don't want headhunters after me, because it would be seen as greed, trying to play both ends against the middle.

"And another thing. Be sensitive about criticism. If you see problems, what do you do? You can fix some on your own. But you usually need your boss's support or other people's help, too. So make your case to your boss carefully. Don't be seen as a critic. Your company feels threatened enough externally by competitors, regulators, the public, and the like. It doesn't need you complaining, too. Your boss needs a team to help solve problems and demonstrate high performance.

"And don't complain outside your unit or to your staff. If you have concerns, just bring them to your boss, constructively. If you campaign for changes, you risk being seen as not a team player. Then you're expendable. I complain here about minority recruitment, training, and promotion, but I'm careful when, how, and to whom. Recently, they eased a white senior guy out. Gave him a nice settlement. But they made it clear he had no future after he complained too loud, too long about problems. Companies and bosses are touchy about criticism they see as disloyalty."

Linda Jackson

"I changed jobs a year ago. My boss and I had different views on what's important. We weren't in sync. We couldn't reach a meeting of the minds on what the job should be. In soft areas, it's hard to figure out what's important and where to concentrate. I've got to meet budget, sales targets, etc. But lots of black managers deal with intangibles that are critical to their evaluation.

"They give you too much to do, then cut your staff. They don't give you enough resources. They feel uncomfortable having you manage lots of people. So they set up these funny reporting systems and strange organizational designs to minimize your leverage and power.

"There's a pattern. You say, 'I need this,' and they say, 'Well, let's try it this way awhile.' A black senior manager was told his staff had to be streamlined because of bottom-line problems. But then he was so constrained, he couldn't do the job. So they let him go. Then much of his job was restructured under his white successor.

"Lots of problems arise from inherited relationships. Mobility undermines the bonding that normally occurs with a boss and with colleagues. Blacks can't move as easily laterally either. So senior black managers work their way up but have trouble moving laterally at high salary in positions that would have many whites reporting to them. So your options are limited, and they can negotiate tougher. There are fewer of us here than five years ago. These folks didn't mess up, and they didn't fail to meet the bottom line. But even if you do well, you still can't move up, even in quantifiable areas—sales, finance, production. And it's harder in softer areas.

"My boss is the CFO. If I send a memo he'd written over his signature, no problem. But if I signed and sent the same memo, I'd get phone calls and questions: 'Is this really what you mean?' It's irritating. Peers my age are running companies. I'm getting annoyed by this whole situation."

Al Crenshaw, 31, works for a Big Six firm. He helps public sector clients on information and financial systems problems.

"I'm quick to defer to superiors' greater experience. I have technical confidence in my training, a BS in engineering and a

Harvard MBA. But I'm new in this field. My boss is more accommodating because I'm black. He's not as likely to criticize, even when I need it.

"A year ago, a white woman, with a reputation for being extremely difficult, hard-nosed, demanding, threatening, was my boss. But I had no problems. She was nice, always joking, not pressing. It never got distasteful. When I'd feel strongly, she'd give in. I was prepared to fight for points. But she'd just laugh if we were headed for disagreement, and give in. I was surprised. She'd had a nasty conflict with another black manager a year before. He charged racism and carried the battle all the way to top management. So that probably had something to do with it. But she'd been scared by that experience, so we didn't have the kind of professional give and take I look for."

Larry Prince, 40, is an investment manager.

"At the foundation, I had been recruited by a finance and administration VP to help move the portfolio into less stodgy areas—real estate, private placements, offshore, etc. I was to help develop the diversification policy. We were to put 10 percent into these higher-risk investments. Then, from being staff, I got operating responsibilities, reporting to the treasurer. He was not in favor of it. He would have preferred I not work for him. I didn't see it as personal. I respected him as a seasoned Wall Street professional.

"Over a couple of years, I worked closely with him. But he and his boss had conflicts. His boss tried to fire him every summer but couldn't. Then he began to see me as a professional in my own right. Gradually I became a member of the team. I showed genuine interest in his expertise. He was a great stock picker. And I respected that. Showing interest helped.

"Investment didn't talk to program guys. We were in investment, but I was interested in the program divisions. So I bridged the cultures and interacted. I also analyzed company social responsibility, and my boss resented that, too. He thought social objectives were irrelevant to investments. But I rolled up my sleeves and learned technique from him. I knew investment theory but not nuts and bolts. So I got involved in what was essentially clerical work. Trading is grunt work.

"He began to see me less as a dilettante—quiche and brie and white wine—and more a meat-and-potatoes guy. I voluntarily gave up my office and moved down to the floor near the action in a big room sharing a desk. They resented I'd had a big office in the first place. So when I was willing to relinquish that short term, to prepare for the long term, that won respect. But after several years this fellow left. My new boss and I never hit it off. He was only five years older, much younger than my former boss. He took some of my functions. I was prepared to support him. But we were never comfortable.

"I was overseeing computerization. We were finally getting state of the art in management information systems. I was well down the path. But he disagreed on approach. That soured the relationship. I couldn't make the concessions I'd made earlier with former bosses. By then I was the senior black manager. I was totally professional. But we forcefully disagreed. We also differed in style. He resented my access to senior officers, and he wanted more deference. It didn't work out."

Mode 3

Brad Graham

"Some whites want to feel they're not racist. And having you around makes them feel okay. Some are just insecure. As a subordinate, you can make them feel whole. But if black managers would share more information, network better, we would all have fewer problems and make fewer missteps.

"I worked for an insecure white woman. She wanted me to be a shrink. But I refused. I toyed with her. But that was a mistake. You can play games. You can say you won't dance to their tune. But they can get you."

Ralph Adams, 50, is a management consultant.

"We studied a new financial product for installment acquisition of businesses. The analysis was competent but unimaginative. But the division that would implement didn't want to. I suggested a pilot project. But my boss said this hadn't been an original option and couldn't be considered. I pushed it and teed him off. But he probably would have accepted a novel idea from a crony.

"I had another boss, brilliant, analytical, insightful. But we disagreed on one project. It got sour. We ended barely speaking. Strong differences can damage relationships. It takes skill to disagree yet get along. Some have it, I don't. Disagreements, for me, turn personal. I've had two instances of raised voices. I got fed up and told them they didn't know their jobs. But that's not the way to work with any boss. This happened with old bureaucrats but wouldn't have with a knowledgeable boss who earned respect.

Jack Davidson, 40, an international economic development consultant, is a lawyer and Harvard MBA.

"Blacks who have done well in first-line general management consulting have been assertive and quick. But their clients only have limited ability to tolerate those qualities in black professionals. So the consultant needs extra skill and balance.

"I was on assignment in Europe. The client was a pulp and paper company. We developed a view of the company and its situation that would threaten many plant managers. And as we moved along, we met resistance. One plant had data we needed, and they knew we knew they had it. The managers withheld it. The project leader and I asked for it. I confronted them. Later, the leader blew up. He said, 'That was my place to bring that issue to a head, not yours. You were out of line.' I said, 'If I were from a European office instead of who I am, would you have this problem?' He admitted, 'No.' So, on that level, subtle differences with superiors show up.

"Another example happened in Africa. I had a contact high in government. I learned of an opportunity worth $1 million in annual fees. But when I presented it at headquarters, instead of saying, 'This is fantastic,' they said, 'You had the audacity to go into this region where we have no projects and no interest? And you think, if we bid and win, you would lead, even though you're a junior. Next time go through channels.'

"I had a different view of my capabilities. That's a common mismatch, not only in professional services but in finance and manufacturing. My boss even told me, 'I like you. You do good work. But you threaten some clients.' That word *threaten* is code for assertive, self-confident, competent.

"Blacks who stay in and move ahead are better at office politics. Those who leave, and especially who go entrepreneurial, are less willing to kiss ass. When I left, the firm made outplacement available. But it didn't work for any black consultants."

Bob York

"My colleagues are heavily quantitative, even when it's not germane. My approach is different. So, in that environment, I sometimes feel insecure. I don't talk for the sake of talking. If I have something to contribute, I do. But people posture. And I sit back. Unfortunately, senior execs evaluate us based on how we posture.

"What I do is important, but I can't do things I really want to do. My boss is lacking in one area. And I said so to the CEO. He said people thought I wasn't playing the game right, that I had my own agenda. So I checked. And others confirmed that was how I was perceived. So I had to become more supportive, get on the team.

"At one point, it looked like I might be terminated because of this. I'll either find something better to do here or be asked to leave. But I'm decisive. My boss is not. He leaves others exposed. And I'm at political odds with him. I can't play the game forever. But none of this has to do with race. He would be the same with anyone with my personality. He should not feel threatened by me, but he seems to be.

"I had a problem with a staffer. I recommended he be fired. But my boss said, 'No. Work with him.' So I did. But he didn't improve. Then, nine months later, my boss says, 'Fire him.' I said, 'No. You fire him, because you delayed and forced me to deal with his incompetence. And I don't want to be a hypocrite now.' I later found out he had asked candidates for employment in my unit, 'How would you like to work for a black man?' Two of those we hired are now social friends. That's how I found out."

6

Getting Ahead

"If you wish in this world to advance
Your merits you're bound to enhance
You must stir it and stump it
And blow your own trumpet
Or, trust me, you haven't a chance."

GILBERT AND SULLIVAN

"I have learned to seek my happiness by limiting my desires,
rather than in attempting to satisfy them."

JOHN STUART MILL

"The trouble with the rat race is that even if you win, you're
still a rat."

LILY TOMLIN

"You can make it if you try."

SLY STONE

There are two major schools of thought about how to get ahead.
Managers who fancy themselves hard-nosed, hard-headed, hardball players say political skill is key. Other managers, who can be
cynical about the idea of a meritocracy, nevertheless emphasize
production and performance. And many subscribe to the two

views, try to balance them, and look to benefit on both merit and political standing.

While it's useful to be aware of the two views, it's equally important to recognize that many senior managers are shifting from the political/social to the meritocratic preference in light of increasing global competition.

What Do Senior Managers Look For?

In most Old Guard companies, personal characteristics have more to do with your rewards, recognition, and advancement than objective performance. The question is: Are you well liked? Personality traits are key. And black managers who are socially skilled do better than those who aren't.

Many books have examined this issue over the decades. In the 1950s, William Whyte told how it was done in *The Organization Man*. Vance Packard examined the process in *The Pyramid Climbers*. And Eugene Jennings' *Executive Success* also shed light on the path to promotion. But what factors are key in *your* company? What's the relative weight of performance, politics, and personality?

Syracuse University management professors Gary Gemmill and Donald DeSalvia surveyed managers to monitor what they value in subordinates. Among the forty qualities most prized, these are some highlights:

Selling Ideas	Understands Peoples' Emotions
Communicating Clearly	Social Background Congruency
Cooperation and Teamwork	Skill at Politics
Respect for Colleagues	Accepts Criticism
Tact with Superiors	Has a Valuable Spouse
Respect of Subordinates	Lives in the Right Place
Has a Sponsor	Looks Like a Manager
Clean-Cut Appearance	Can Disagree with Bosses
Has a Promotable Superior	

That's reality. But all these qualities, more so than the ones we omitted, have a potential racial angle. All are subjective. And all have cultural values built in that can work against you. So it will pay to strengthen your weak areas, wherever possible.

Robert Half, based on his survey of personnel directors, emphasizes the importance of showing a sense of humor. You'll be perceived as more creative, less rigid, and more open to new ideas. But racial realities often generate anger and diminish good humor—another catch-22. *Reacting* to injustice, arrogance, and incompetence generates more injustice and makes you appear a sorehead, and that limits your rewards and promotability.

There are 412 generals in the U.S. Army. Only twenty-five of them (6 percent) are African Americans. Studies say the military offers better management opportunities for African Americans that the private sector. That may be true marginally. But issues of your loyalty and perceived threat as a change agent can cause resistance in both sectors. To be promoted, rewarded, and recognized, produce and fit your company's culture. That takes energy, good health, and stamina. Being able to survive and hang in there is another key to getting promoted.

Bosses want subordinates to be satisfied and fulfilled. But that's not an end in itself. It's instrumental. When you're not satisfied, it keeps you from helping your boss meet her objectives. The company's interests and yours are often not the same. Only when they are will you get what you think you deserve.

What You Can Do

First Do No Harm

To get consistent recognition, prove yourself to your boss, colleagues, and others. Approach work the way the Hippocratic Oath guides medical practice. Its first requirement—do no harm—is also good management practice. To get promoted, recognized, and rewarded, first don't foul up. Do the little things well. After that, go for the home runs.

Don't break simple local customs and rules. Respect the culture. Don't rush into high-risk projects. Do routine housekeeping—filling out forms, for example—properly.

Impress Your Boss

Another key, discussed in chapter 5, is to be well thought of by your boss for both tangible and intangible reasons. You can get rewards and promotions on sheer craftsmanship without a solid relationship, or even with one that's hostile. But that's harder.

The University of Michigan's Alfred W. Swinyard and Floyd A. Bond believe you need a good graduate school education from a "top" school. And they stress experience in operations, finance, and marketing. Get varied experience in assignments important to your bosses.

Follow a Plan

What about a written, updated career strategy? Without one, you can end up spinning your wheels or getting sidetracked.

Michael Driver, who teaches at the University of Southern California, has noticed four career patterns.

Steady state—committed to developing and refining skills and a specialty and to building a reputation and expertise.

Linear—committed to climbing within a hierarchical organization. You're likely to plateau with this strategy.

Transitory—job hopping.

Spiral—a series of careers and major shifts, such as radical changes from business to music to farming.

These categories illuminate broad strategy options. To figure out where you really belong and what styles suit you best, go to a first-rate career counseling firm and personally pay for their tests and interviews. Make this investment. Much complaint about "ceilings" comes from people who find themselves in the wrong specialty, the wrong industry, or the wrong company. They're not using available career development tools. If you're in accounting but should be in sales or human resources, you're mismatched, and your miseries probably have little to do with race.

Good counselors will help you understand your style, learn more about yourself, and become aware and fully conscious. That will help you plan and execute your strategy.

Choose and Concentrate

Does your company track promotable managers? More and more systematically track talent? This increases objectivity and reduces racial influences. But too many companies promote with little attention to performance records. Decisions are often seat-of-the-pants, based on favoritism, seniority, cronyism, and race.

Now, computers force human resource managers to better define skills needed by the company. That helps identify your weaknesses, and where you need training and growth assignments. It also helps identify the skills you've concentrated on and mastered. You'll benefit from this increased sophistication and objectivity. You're more likely to be stalled, wasted, plateaued, or misused than Yammies and Old Boys, so better information systems will help decision makers discover you and help you get out from under anyone impeding you.

Job hopping—seemingly unplanned, opportunistic, poorly handled moves—gives a poor impression. But you gain specific skills and experience by planned, careful job moves. You may be tempted to say yes to attractive job opportunities with little regard for how they fit your strategy. That's how most managers move. Long-range planning sounds good. It's rational and professional. Do it, even though it's difficult and seems abstract.

Dress for Success

Don't expect rewards while dressing out of line. Conform to the standards in your firm and industry. Some managers defend individualism as a sign of racial spirit, a way not to sell your soul. That's nonsense. Wear the uniform of your company. If you don't, don't complain if you're penalized. Fashion nonconformity is not a good way to assert integrity and make a statement.

Look the way promotables in your industry and company look. The Directory of Personal Image Consultants can suggest firms that will help you refine personal presentation. Or simply observe your world, talk to savvy friends, and save consulting fees.

Sound and act the part. Pick people who "have it" as role models. Gestures, posture, and eye contact all contribute or detract. Image becomes more important as managers deal more with the media. You'll meet the press and television as you move up. If you're good at that, you're more promotable.

Find Inherent Satisfaction

Do you feel fulfilled? Have you found the right team, and are you fairly paid, rewarded, and recognized? If so, you won't leave just for more money. Only greater challenges will lure you. Show what you can do. Make the most of your skills. That's the reward.

What are the probabilities for promotion? Ask yourself these questions:

- Is a promotion, an interesting lateral move, or an expanded current role possible within, say, two years?
- Are you seen as a doer, on the fast track and promotable?
- Is your personal relationship with your boss good?
- Do you feel well paid?
- Have you been in your job over two years?
- Have you been passed over unfairly for promotion?
- Is your work load too light or too heavy?
- Do you get along with your coworkers?
- Are you adequately plugged in to the informal politics?

Too many negative answers, and you're not in good shape for rewards. But you can always find intrinsic merit in the job and contribute.

Be Mobile

You're doing a good job, getting to know the right people, protecting your flanks, finding inherent satisfaction, looking over your shoulder, and avoiding the games. But in addition to race, if you were born between 1946 and 1960, you have another problem. You are part of the baby boom, and you'll be impeded or blocked by older managers and by demographics as much as by racial politics.

To move ahead against demographic and racial odds, move more frequently. Average two years rather than three. Work more intensely to cram equivalent experience into the time.

Let's say you're in a consumer goods company. You finish the management training program, then look to an early assignment as an assistant product manager. After two years or so, you expect to move to product manager. Then, after two or three years, it might be strategic planning or new product development. And five to ten years after that, when you're around forty years old, group product manager might be the next slot.

About here is where race might enter. If you planned well and dedicated yourself, you would expect to be considered for vice president. To get those rewards and promotions, you need some political skill. And check the market with headhunters you've cultivated.

Gene Dalton and Paul Thompson's *Novations: Strategies for Career Development* describes four career stages: apprentice, colleague, master, and director.

- As an *apprentice* you learn, follow directions, and do detailed routine work.
- As a *colleague* you become independent, specialize, and become expert and credible.
- As a *mentor* you broaden, become a leader, and deal with people outside your company.
- As a *director* you help determine strategy and represent your firm in senior negotiations.

At each stage you should renegotiate your duties and opportunities with superiors. To move ahead, you need new agreements on relationships and obligations. But many managers don't handle the transitions well, and that's why they get stuck.

Negotiate at formal *and* informal performance reviews. Talk about training, assignments, promotions, and other opportunities. Mention your ambitions and review what's going *for* and *against* you. And when opportunities come along for interviews that might lead to promotion:

- *Do your homework* on the new unit's business issues, culture, philosophy, and key personalities.
- *Keep the conversation on point* and avoid trivia and digressions.
- *Be natural* and let the interviewer set the tone and pace.
- *Don't be negative.* Talk about opportunities and solutions, not problems.
- *Use the interview to learn* about the real details of the situation, not just superficial issues.

Know When Not to Accept an Offer

Somewhere along the line, you'll have an opportunity to be promoted or lateraled to a job that's not quite what you were looking for. It has some attractions, but it's in the wrong location. Or it's out of your specialty. Or maybe it's window dressing, or a dead end—more money, big title, perks, but not on the track of your plan.

Think hard if the only reason you hesitate is relocation. If you're asked to relocate, it's probably a positive sign, even though you may not want to. The average cost of moving you is $30,000, so a request to relocate—even to the boondocks—means you're valued.

The Korn Ferry search consulting firm says the average senior executive moves three times in a career. If you decline, don't be negative about the assignment or the location. Be positive, explaining that the timing, location, or assignment is less attractive than your present job. But moving up will almost certainly mean moving someday, and then you'll need to make lifestyle decisions.

Find a Need and Fill It

Expand your scope. Look into other areas for broader experience. But take care not to offend anyone or step on toes. Look for problems outside your area that are undefined and untreated—and help solve them.

Some people will resent your mere existence. And they'll grumble if you expand your scope. But go ahead. Take on challenges. Enrich your experience. Don't wait for responsibility. And even if you contribute, you may still get little recognition or reward, especially in Old Guard companies. But you benefit by stretching.

Good work is its own reward. And, in most firms, despite racism, good work is valued. Whether you get rewards as quickly or from the same sources as Yammies and Old Boys do is another question. But talent, application, thoughtfulness, and hard work pay off, if not where you are now, then someplace else later.

Achieve Concrete Goals That Bear Your Name

Heidrick and Struggles, and Korn Ferry, leading management recruiters, regularly survey to spot trends in promotion patterns. In the 1980s, more production/operations types moved to the top and bypassed finance and marketing specialists. Document your contributions. And make some difference in the outcome that others recognize. If you save money by cutting costs, that's a concrete contribution. Look for ways to do that. Pay attention to economic realities in your unit. Help improve them.

Thomas Deal and Anthony Kennedy's book *Corporate Cultures* predicts "no-boss" environments. You won't waste time worrying about how to get rewards, recognition, and promotions, and how to climb the rigging, because there won't *be* any rigging. That kind of environment should be more amenable to people who want to accomplish something tangible they can take pride in. And it should be less racially biased, since there'll be less room for manipulation and cronyism.

Promote yourself. Many managers find that distasteful, and they hate to do it, and hate to see others doing it. But do it with integrity by citing concrete accomplishments. You're working uphill against opposition: So use personal PR. When you complete an important project: *Get published.* Write work-related articles for business and professional journals. And *get on news or talk shows to discuss professional and business issues.* Let producers and directors of shows in your area know you're available.

You may feel your good work and relations with colleagues and bosses should be enough. But it can't hurt to toot your own horn, tastefully. Find dignified ways to put your name in front of the right audiences. It's important in getting full and proper rewards.

Don't Bang Your Head on the Ceiling

Norman J. Hill is an African-American corporate director of personnel operations at Burger King. He says, "We can't afford to turn down talent, wherever it's found. No smart businessman is going to cut himself off from 20 percent of the talent market simply because of something like skin color."

But clearly, that's not true. Managers make selections based on what they feel is the natural and proper social order of things, and that involves racial loyalties and preferences. The real test of talent is the perception that you could help a competitor take market share or increase profits. When you are seen that way, ceilings will be lifted. Until then, they'll remain.

Wendell L. Johnson consults on career issues. He says African Americans hit a barrier at middle management. "Many either leave voluntarily or are literally forced out because there's no room up." Ceilings differ by industry, function, and region, as well as within your particular company. It's hard to spot barriers from outside looking in. So talk to other black managers. Ask if there's opportunity for them to move up, and why and why not.

Blue Chips and High Drafts (see p. 22) can move more easily. Low Drafts and Free Agents can be mobile early in their careers but tend to settle for security as they become aware of limitations, relative disadvantages, and job market realities.

When you hit a ceiling, either accept that reality and concentrate on the craft, or move to where you'll be recognized and rewarded. Don't waste time arguing injustices. By the time you hit your ceiling, you've made enemies and chalked up scores to settle. Old Boys and Yammies will be lying in ambush. So save yourself aggravation. Gracefully move to greener pastures.

Don't be too disappointed if you're blocked for reasons you can't figure out. Don't settle in too emotionally with *any* company. Be prepared to leave. Take your accumulated skills, knowledge, experience, and record of documented contributions and achievements, to your next employer, where you will have a clean slate and no immediate enemies.

Understand the culture, values, beliefs, and rituals in your company. Do you fit? Perhaps. But as you approach the ceiling, typically at the top of middle management, mismatches in values and beliefs become significant. And these factors stymie upward movement.

You can get opportunities to be treated fairly and to get rewards, promotions, and respect by moving from a larger to a smaller company. But race can be even trickier there. In smaller companies, there are fewer buffers. You have to fit the culture and find the right chemistry with key people, and if there's a cultural snag, it's likely your only option is to leave. But in a big company, you can find other departments where the fit is better and the rewards and recognition for good performance can be more objectively based.

Work With Headhunters

Can headhunters help you get ahead? Pay attention to how they operate, and cultivate one or two.

Ted Weaver, an executive recruiter who has placed many black middle and junior level managers, believes that "often black potential candidates are reluctant to respond to headhunters. Lots of times, black people have been worked over in the recruiting process. They've been used. So they react cautiously when I call.

"Various companies, over the years, have played games. I had a client in the computer industry. They wanted special kinds of people, they said. Freethinkers. Not IBM regimented types. It was tough recruiting for them. The chemistry between candidates and each manager had to be just right. Politically, it was a jungle. You had to be able to skip through an electric fan to be successful in that company.

"The founder had a bias against Catholics, which, incidentally, I am. My friend in personnel was Catholic, and he knew he'd never make VP. But they swore up and down they weren't prejudiced.

"I put several black guys in there for them. A manufacturing guy, an electrical engineer, a woman in personnel. They spent a lot of money on search but hired only a few. After three or four years, I was retained to find a black purchasing agent. They said there were no black purchasing agents who had manufacturing backgrounds. I listened to the human resource guy. He complained, 'I'll find ten or fifteen candidates. Then the line guys will find reasons why they're not compatible.' I had talked to a black guy who said, 'This company doesn't want us.' But I went ahead and found people. Then it turned out there was a racist in purchasing vetoing the candidates. Finally, top management figured out the purchasing guy was the problem, not that there weren't qualified candidates. They apologized and said it had caused trouble before. But they caught the guy red-handed on this one.

"I used to be sensitive about being labeled a 'minority recruiter.' I just wanted to be a recruiter. But I don't feel that way anymore. Now, I'm glad to do it, because if I don't, who will?"

When a headhunter calls, turn over the stone. It doesn't cost anything to talk. Probe the situation being presented. If the recruiter is white, he or she may not be sensitive about the souls of black folks or aware of what black managers have been through in these recruiting and promotion games the last fifteen years, so don't assume they'll know what's important to you. But black recruiters may not know enough about the situations they're presenting, either.

Be realistic. Headhunters like to get resumés in the mail—but, frankly, only if you've been to the "right" schools, have the "right" experience, and are the "right" age for what you're looking for. And you know if you're right and have the right credentials. A lot of folks reach beyond realistic expectations when looking to move.

Headhunters *do* like to meet new people, especially if they think you might be a potential source of business. So nurture contacts with headhunters. Keep in touch with one or two. Drop them notes and items on yourself—but not in excess. And offer to help with their searches.

Network

Procter & Gamble, Xerox, McKinsey, GE, and other large companies have alumni networks that help professionals and managers throughout their careers. If your company has a former-employees network, join after you leave. If you left with a bad taste, wait until the anger subsides, then join. These groups may be formal or informal, and they may be recognized by the company or not. But they offer useful contacts.

Know How to Handle an Interview

When you're in an interview, you'll get questions such as:

- Why do you want this job?
- Can you tell me about your boss?
- What are your strengths and weaknesses?
- What do you like about your job?
- What achievements are you proud of?
- Where do you want to be in five years?

Be prepared. Show you're thoughtful. Make your goals, likes, and dislikes clear. Don't bad-mouth a previous or current boss, but make clear what kind of boss and what kind of situation you're comfortable with. Also, don't confess major weaknesses—but don't try to look perfect, either. Own up to minor defects. Say what you feel. Don't tell interviewers what you *think* they want to hear.

Be logical and straight, not tentative and unsure. Choose how you want to come across, and make the impressions you want to make. Don't wing it.

Take Stock of Your Professional Needs

If you're looking to make a move, ask yourself:

- What's my motivation? Is it just money, or do I want more responsibilities?
- How good are my formal credentials? Do I need to add training or pick up a special skill?
- How's my current company's reputation? Is it profitable, competitive, and growing?
- Have I been in this slot long enough? Have I made a definite contribution that I can document? Have I been moving upward, or am I stuck?
- Am I on track for my age and experience? How appropriate is my compensation?

Check your positioning, timing, readiness, and motivation.

Be Realistic in Negotiations

How much should you expect when changing jobs? The inducements aren't as sweet as they were in the 1970s. Thirty to 50 percent increases were more common then. But 20 to 30 percent is possible in the 1990s.

When you ask about bonuses, promotions, raises, assignments, and perks, be candid but tactful. You'll get candid answers if you think about your approach and are respectful. But too much caution will keep you from exploring all the sensitive aspects of the situation. And if you avoid those, sooner or later you'll begin to resent your company and your boss, and it will be reciprocated. Bargain for responsibility, resources, adequate compensation, relocation assistance, and other normal and helpful benefits. But skip the requests for the unusual that you heard others get.

If you're in middle management, you probably have not thought you needed or could get a contract or severance agreement. But middle managers who have bargaining leverage can get contracts and agreements. If you have a strong position, you may do better than the traditional agreement when you go into a new situation, or even in your current one.

You can ask for, and get, severance agreements, money, outplacement help, and bonuses, agreed to up front. You might be able to get an agreement on three, six, or even twelve months' salary as severance. If you earn over $80,000, you're in the range where agreements may be available.

If a headhunter comes after you, you're probably in a position to talk about a contract or a letter of agreement. But the number of calls from search firms for African-American managers fluctuates. The trouble is, black managers still often tend to go in "on a humble." Know your strength. Take the market's temperature every year, at least, so you know your value. Don't feel flattered by attention.

Turn Setbacks Into Learning Experiences

Many successful executives have been fired sometime along the way, not for incompetence but because of a personality mismatch. If it happens, what do you do? After you account for whatever racial angles you know or imagine were involved, concentrate on turning the experience to your advantage.

Since race is a dimension, your normal anger is potentially even more explosive. But be diplomatic, so you set the stage for seeking references and favorable terms for separation. It's asking a lot, but make the incident a basis for growth and progress. Don't tell your boss you consider him a racist. Instead, reflect, seek opinions on how you were perceived, see if you can learn from the events leading up to the firing, and make adjustments based on that feedback.

Take the opportunity to reevaluate your career and strategy. Maybe you should be in a different field or should be your own boss. You'll have lots of company if you arrive at that conclusion. The main thing is, despite racism, use setbacks to help you get ahead.

The Modes and How They View
Getting Ahead

Mode 1 managers say work hard and produce quality, but politics, networking, and maneuvering are more important. It's who you know. They see few outright, and only minimal institutional impediments. And they see whites as essentially benign and neutral.

Mode 2 managers say getting ahead requires balancing production and politics. They see more opposition to advancement and see whites as sometimes an obstacle.

Mode 3 managers say pure hard work and results are key. Politics can easily backfire or make you lose focus or make enemies. They see a great deal of institutional and personal opposition, and they see whites as often an obstacle.

All three modes recognize racial barriers. The differences are in degree and in what they emphasize regarding how to reach goals and deal with impediments.

Mode 1

Jack Bell

"Blacks who make it here do what's needed. Sell your soul. Play the game. Some try that, but in two or three years they're gone anyhow.

"Cut the umbilical cord to your own culture and become part of theirs, and you can get ahead without outstanding ability. The best blacks don't necessarily rise. But I want my son to work here. I can tell and show him how to become president. I just couldn't do it myself. I was on a rocket but was asked to relocate at a crucial time in my family's life. My boss said I should take it or it would be like starting over. I would have been the youngest black marketing manager in the company. But that refusal killed me.

"Later, I had another shot. A boss was trying to mentor, but I didn't realize it. I was cocky and stupid. But even with these disappointments, this is still a great company.

"Success requires more savvy than it used to. I've seen tremendous change in attitudes. Reagan affected the climate. See that young guy walking by? Sharp. He can make VP in ten years. He handles himself well, and he listens. I talk to young blacks, but too many are busy finger popping. They won't listen."

Ben Pringle

"Politics counts for 65 percent of achieving what you want. Skill, delivery, and execution, 25 percent, and luck, 10 percent. I should have played more politics. I was under the false impression the percentages were reversed. If I'd known, I could have done less work, missed deliverables, and still got promoted. I was too up-front. And I could have gotten ahead by being liked by the right people.

"Have a good relationship with your supervisor. Then get to know senior executives. And your boss will think, 'This dude's plugged in,' and he'll deal with you differently. That's protection so you don't get lost in the shuffle.

"One black guy got no rewards, no recognition, and was released for no apparent reason. He didn't get along. Instead of being creative, he developed an attitude. And that justified releasing him. His boss was a racist. I worked for him later. He should have handled it like I did. When I was assigned, I said, 'What are we trying to do next quarter?' And he gave me some textbook answer. I said, 'I'll do my best to make you look good. I'll scratch your back and help you so you'll take care of me later.' And this guy, who couldn't stand niggers, worked well with me. He loved me. I wouldn't let anything upset me. And when he acted ignorant and made comments about affirmative action or other issues, I'd get the subject back on priorities. Let 'social science' remarks pass. Stay focused. 'I'm here to help you and do a job.'

"Don't contradict overtly. And know where he stands politically and whether he's going anywhere. Read the political winds. And if he's about to make a mistake, distance. Talk to him. Listen. Know where his head's at. Stay close. Too many blacks distance.

"When I was overseas, every three months I wrote to one executive. And I'd stop by, when at headquarters, to tell him what I was doing. I'd mention my boss favorably and say, 'I'm learning a lot, and growing, and like this assignment.' And he'd drop by my office to say hello. And my boss would ask, 'What's that about?'

"My brother followed my advice at his company. He got to know the chairman, CEO, and COO. They invited him to visit, and he took advantage. But he summarized the meetings and showed his notes to his boss so he'd know they'd asked for input and it wasn't an end run. His boss, the director of planning, hadn't wanted him initially, so this fortunate opportunity was protection. His boss sent reports to the Executive Committee. My brother convinced the president and COO to let his boss present rather than simply send reports. But his boss preferred to let him present. So the top people got to see his work."

Adele Belmont

"A black EEO vice president told me I wasn't paid comparably to a white colleague and suggested I challenge. I said no. I'd leave to work where I'd be paid appropriately, not where I had to fight for assignments and rewards.

"One guy at my level had a better political game—tennis and racquetball with the boss. But that wasn't open to me. Now I work for a black vice president. He told me what he expected. I've done it. And I'm evaluated fairly and rewarded."

Jerry Elliott, 48, is in government relations for a major manufacturer.

"Tell your boss you want growth and responsibilities. But don't talk about leaving unless you have a firm offer. Then ask what he plans for you. You'll be in a better position to get commitments.

"A company I'd talked to approached our general manager. This put pressure on my boss. But we talked about my job's scope and working conditions. He made adjustments, and I stayed. But the key was performance. He didn't want to lose me."

Mode 2

Alan Roland, 52, is an engineer and senior manager in aerospace.

"Progress depends more on trust and luck than ability. In fact, the smartest people don't rise. People who are trusted, whose superiors are comfortable with them and understand them, rise."

Joe Wilson

"I was frustrated, biding my time. I saw people above me I didn't consider in my class. The funnel is small for anybody. But white seniors look for similar types. They find it tough to pick blacks for top jobs. They have to be secure. So black people are likely to get to senior management only in companies with troubles, like this one. Now there's a pool, more than a handful, in general management. So it's not unrealistic to expect five to ten CEOs in the next ten years."

Ossie Gordon

"My boss didn't think I had administrative skill, so I wasn't slated for senior partner, managing partner.

"You need a mentor, and I didn't have one, so my future was constrained, even though I was making $200,000. Between thirty and forty, you don't mind working like crazy. You can run like hell. But at fifty, you don't want to. To get rewards, you have to push $1 million a year in billings and run a lot of projects. And there's no time for anything else. Forget balance.

"Now I enjoy being an entrepreneur. I'm not scared anymore. But at the firm, I was scared a lot. 'Will I get this done in time?' You constantly had to prove yourself. And if you got into management, you had to relocate, go where you're asked, or you weren't playing the game."

Louise Gibson

"I reported to an SVP. He had us for dinner, from time to time, where it was kosher to talk about women's problems, but not blacks'.

"And I had a mentor, an EVP. He pushed women. He said to my boss, 'Move her. And if you don't, I will.' He seeded the organization with his people. He may have gained at the board level by sponsoring women. He asked me for input for a board discussion on blacks. The bank hires lots of entry-level blacks. But attrition is staggering, 80 percent. And the question was, is it the bank or the people?

"I wasn't seen as black. It wasn't explicit, but I could tell. I was on the fast track. But in a way, I was also held back. I was a threat because of class issues—prep school, etc. I knew I had to be on somebody's team. You have to get pulled along. If that doesn't happen, you get stuck early. Then many blacks leave.

"I had a timetable. If the bank didn't move me by a certain date, I'd look outside. I was burned out anyhow. About that time, they promoted two white guys I was outperforming. Then they outearned me by $50,000 in base pay. So I talked to head-hunters, and if the bank found out, that was all right.

"When I left, they said, 'Come back anytime.' So I left in a strong position. Friends I made in early career have paid off. They stay in touch, and several gave my name to headhunters. My resumé used to indicate I was black. Later, I took that off. I show growth in responsibilities, and breadth in functions. And I allude to outside activities. I don't assume things are stacked against me. Too many blacks do."

Pat Halman, 50, worked in retailing.

"I add responsibilities rather than try for promotions. In hard times, work can be eliminated. Make yourself less expendable by expanding functions."

Frank Reynolds, 48, is a SVP of a midsize East Coast bank.

"I was in over my head when I joined. I started collecting delinquent loans. I stumbled into finance, did well, and got rapid promotions every two years. I moved from lending to operations to credit analysis to human resources to government and community affairs to guaranteed lending within ten years.

"When offered a job, take it even if you feel unqualified. Let them decide. Work hard and master it. I took assignments beyond me. I learned branch administration on the job. I didn't know the technical side. So I was humble. I didn't try to fake it. Know your limitations. Use staff talents. Let them know you respect them. I promote good people. That builds loyalty."

Mode 3

Carl Wilson

"People look out for their own. A black guy complained that his boss brought in a white guy over him. I told him he'd brought in his right-hand man and was looking out for him. That's not race, per se.

"White people don't think about you unless you're visible. How do you get visibility? Produce great results. When you want something, they look at performance first. If your numbers aren't there, forget it."

Bill Tompkins works in computer marketing.

"To get promoted, I work my buns off. Does affirmative action work for me? No. I earned it. There's lip service to developing minorities, but that's all.

"Formal mentors don't exist here. You develop a mentor on your own. We're lean. We go for the gusto. The bottom line. Of course, the president may hire an outstanding minority and create a slot. But employers want Harvard Business School types. Well, that excludes 99 percent of the potential people who could do the job. Most companies don't develop the blacks they do hire. I'm as successful as anyone could be who's not brilliant or in a crucial technical specialty."

Henry Clapton, 49, is a bank vice president in California.

"Decide how long you'll stay. Have a departure date in mind when you sign on. Learn skills or a new subject to take with you. Don't change jobs out of dissatisfaction. Move on *your* timetable. Leave shortly after a promotion or salary increase. You'll compound the increases. And you'll reinforce in your own mind that you're marketable and independent."

Rod Clark, 47, an engineer with his own business, had been a senior manager at a large electronics company in California.

"Recognition, rewards, and promotions are limited because white superiors lack confidence in blacks' abilities. When you're up for promotion, they'll sidetrack it this way: 'Joe's not ready, but he has potential. I like Joe and want him to grow and not fail, so let's train him a little longer.' "

7

Leading From Your Strength

"I have nothing to offer but blood, toil, tears, and sweat."

WINSTON CHURCHILL

"I'm just a stubborn kind of fellow."

MARVIN GAYE

We hear often that black managers will change business by being more "in touch" with their own and their staffs' feelings and deep motivations. As leaders, they'll help humanize organizations. They'll innovate out of personal and cultural experience and will be intuitive and sensitive. They will be "natural," righteous leaders.

All leaders' habits of mind, expectations, and responses are culturally based. But there are plenty of bull-in-the-china-shop black managers. There's not much evidence of natural leadership advantages.

Leading people who are ambivalent about the fact that you have authority depends on more than formal position, rank, title, and technical mastery. Your personality, record, reputation, and ability to build relationships are key. Your social capital accumulates or diminishes, day by day. Choose how and when to invest it carefully.

As we move into the "next economy," information- and knowledge-based organizations will be transformed. Staff participation and involvement will become more important. Hierarchy will be an anachronism. And formal authority will be even more ambiguous. Leadership will be increasingly based on personal qualities, technical mystery, organizational savvy, political skill, and self-awareness. Formal position and title will matter less. Staff members will often be as talented, knowledgeable, and experienced as their superiors. So managers will need to be extremely sensitive to status incongruence.

Many observers see black managers as individualistic leaders. They're often thought to be confrontational, "in your face," idiosyncratic, even quirky, loose cannons, brash, outspoken, rambunctious, unpredictable, and freewheeling, especially in Old Guard organizations.

You can be an individualistic leader if you've built a solid track record. But even if you're very good, notice the experience of someone like John Z. De Lorean, who said that GM doesn't tolerate individualism, that individualists are "rebuked, ordered to disappear into the wallpaper." Iacocca, at Ford, was also creative. But he, too, was ultimately punished. If you stand out, or bug people by marching to a different drummer, or by offering a different vision of where the organization ought to go or of how it ought to get there, expect to be a target.

What You Can Do

Old Boys and Yammies can tolerate you and can want to help you meet objectives. But they can have trouble if you lead and help determine objectives. How can you lead effectively in these circumstances? That's the next hurdle, now that entry opportunities are secured.

Know Yourself, and Be Aware of What You're Doing

How can you overcome resentment and subtle tests of your patience and skill? If you're effective, subordinates will generally not resist. Demonstrate technical competence. That gives you basic credibility.

You are leading in a time of stress and high competition. Automation, international competition, and strong/weak dollar factors require companies to be lean and keen. So lead by adding value—through sales, cutting costs, research, product or program development, operations—or be efficient and creative in a staff function.

Otto Lerbinger and Nathaniel Sperber's *Key to the Executive Head* reports a survey that found that leadership requires *integrity, accepting responsibility, achievement orientation,* and *reliability.* Getting along and fitting in were further down the list. Get along and fit in, obviously, but emphasize performance, even if it's not rewarded fully. You'll get rewards intrinsically now and tangibly later in your career.

To lead effectively you need faith in your ability. Second, develop a quality staff. Then let them help set objectives and emphasize their autonomy.

John Naisbett and Patricia Aburdene's *Reinventing the Corporation* forecasts democratization, shared decision making, *intra*preneurship, and lateral organization replacing hierarchy. You may have an advantage in these new circumstances. The civil rights movement helped accelerate this trend. And you will do better in such environments than in Old Guard, mechanistic ones, because diversity, unorthodoxy, and liberal values will be more welcome, including differences in leadership style. The same authors see corporations tending toward egalitarianism. Leading in Vanguard environments will mean more room for styles "outsiders" bring.

To lead effectively, they suggest you follow this advice:

- Call people by first names.
- Don't use executive parking and restrooms.

- Answer your own phone.
- Seek out people who are simpatico.
- Reduce hierarchy.
- Develop all your team members' skills.
- Reward good work.
- Provide autonomy.
- Respect team members as individuals.

Arnold Mitchell's *The Nine American Lifestyles* forecasts that leaders will give greater weight to social factors in leading. Leaders with deep commitments to social justice and to business, community, and environmental responsibility will have an edge. They'll be more effective and rewarded. Mitchell said we are heading into a period in which Americans will want "the real thing"—authentic, direct, simple lifestyles and leadership styles. Skip pretense and posturing, and you'll come out ahead. Integrity and inner-directedness will be key to leadership.

Traditionally, black managers found greater opportunities in the public sector in the 1940s and 1950s because corporate entry was blocked. Public managers often are motivated by a desire to serve the public interest and produce social change. But that also often characterizes black corporate managers. If you're interested in change, justice, and reform, lead with an overarching purpose beyond mere advancement, bonuses, recognition, and perks.

Be an Activist

Howard Stevenson, a professor at Harvard Business School who studies entrepreneurship, says leadership has to do with situations more than with individual personality. He sees a spectrum of management types, running from activist promoters to passive "trustees." Since you likely want change in organizational traditions, less hierarchy, and more room to innovate, you're probably less a trustee than many Old Boys, satisfied with the status quo.

Tom Peters and Nancy Austin in their book *A Passion for Ex-*

cellence say managers are too focused on rational assumptions, quantitative analysis, and hard justification in decision making. You gain an advantage if you are more intuitive, improvisational even. Trust your intuitive, authentic leadership style.

Be Alert to New Ideas

Keep yourself open to change. Create an open atmosphere so your staff can achieve mutually agreed-upon objectives and satisfy their yearning to make a mark.

You've followed changing fashions in leadership: Management by Objectives, Theory Y, Management by Walking Around, One-Minute Managing, Theory Z, Japanese-style management, Tender Management, Tough Management, etc. Much of the search for all-purpose answers reflects leaders' lack of clear commitment to basic values in dealing with people. With no deep beliefs about how to lead, they try fads, rather than what they believe is right. Know where you stand, and why, and you won't need fads.

Pay attention to the state of the art in organizational development. Old Boys often look askance at OD. It's touchy-feely, soft, liberal, not tough enough. You should know better. Recognize the value of organizational transformation, which is based on participative, gain-sharing, nonhierarchical management. The first principle is that as a leader, you serve your staff. Enable them, and you'll succeed as a unit.

Intel's Andrew Grove says companies should be hybrids. They should be organized by function, and by product or market or mission. Finance, marketing, and production can add to overall efficiency according to how well they're managed. But units devoted to particular products or regions need flexibility, a local detailed touch, and knowledge based on quick feedback from markets about competitors and technological changes. And leaders unburdened by old dogmas are needed to cope.

Middle managers are key. They run production, sales, logistics, personnel, public and community relations, accounts receivables and payables, planning, and other nitty-gritty offices. Grove says they spend too much time writing reports, and that hinders their ability to lead and improve their function. Avoid trivia. Concentrate on what means most to ultimate output. Where is your *leverage*? Think in these terms, and you'll lead successfully.

Robert W. Keidel's *Game Plans: Sports Strategies for Business* derives management metaphors from sports. *Football* is controlled, risk-averse, programmed, and planned—but managers often use a football coach's mode. *Basketball* is fluid, played by generalists with less role specialization, and has more instantaneous adjustments. Keidel suggests paying attention to basketball and avoiding the football coach's mentality.

We are entering a time when leaders need to be flexible and adjust quickly. This may give you an edge if there is a cultural preference for spontaneity, improvisation, and intuitive managers over managers who use the football model.

Hayes and Abernathy blamed the problems of American corporations, among other things, on MBAs who manage by the numbers and give too little attention to the human side. Many black managers are attuned to human issues because of a sensitivity to injustices. That enhances their ability to lead and produce results in Vanguard firms, but it produces resentment from peers in Old Guard companies, who see it as disloyalty.

Anthony Athos and Richard Pascal's *The Art of Japanese Management* was misread by many and unfairly criticized for touting Japanese styles. Their point was, when American managers integrate human and economic values, as many Japanese do, we perform better.

In Wickham Skinner's *Manufacturing: The Formidable Competitive Weapon* we can find another insight about managers who tend to focus on mechanistic productivity—cutting costs and squeezing more output out of people and machines. But, Skinner says, leaders in the new competitive environment will concentrate instead on quality, service, quick delivery, fast new product development, and reliability. Respond to the market, especially if you're in production and operations. Lead according to these new realities.

Build a Loyal Team

Jim Treybig's method at Tandem Computers is one good way to lead: generate intense loyalty, create a culture almost like a cult, give wide personal latitude for creativity and initiative, and use generous perks, rewards, and recognition. You don't need charisma, or even a highly participative progressive style, to stimulate commitment. But they help. Tandem's style can work even in traditional cultures.

To build loyalty even in a bureaucratic Old Guard culture, stick to your own standards. Emphasize staff's dignity. Earn respect and trust, and you'll build loyalty. Guard against tendencies to be rigid, controlling, doctrinaire, authoritarian, and bureaucratic.

On the other hand, you can be too accommodating, democratic, and participative. Some staff members may try to take advantage. Your staff wants you to be fair, decisive, consistent, knowledgeable, and friendly. See people and situations as they really are. Be participative and people-centered, but don't be a soft touch for the manipulators or shirkers.

Since you're African American, you're already different. So conform where you can, but remember, the race factor gives you an advantage in building loyalty, ironically, by freeing you to lead from the soul.

Many Old Boys and Yammies move up and acquire needless and ostentatious class-conscious trappings of office—luxury cars and extravagant social and club arrangements. But conspicuous perks help undermine leadership and loyalty. This drive by executives to differentiate themselves according to status hierarchies unrelated to real contributions and merit is one reason for American underperformance; it breeds resentment.

Less is more. Go for quality and efficiency, not pomp and grade distinctions. Well-run Vanguard companies avoid ostentation. Opt for simplicity, and your ability to lead—not to impress—will be enhanced.

Some black managers are too egalitarian, too Mode 3, afraid to fully use authority. They want to be "one of the boys." They bend over backwards to avoid seeming like the boss. That's not leadership. Be progressive, participative, and collegial, but still be comfortable using authority.

You want staff members to be frank with you, trust you, and take prudent risks without worrying that you might overreact. So level with them, trust and respect them, and be scrupulously fair. Keep a sense of justice in all dealings.

Leaders need timely, accurate, candid feedback from subordinates. But most leaders don't get it, so they don't know where they stand. Subordinates may be afraid to level, and race can heighten that fear. So ask repeatedly for feedback. If you're authentic, you'll benefit. Have those conversations at breakfast or lunch or after work, when you can relax and hear them. Even if what you hear makes you uncomfortable, think about it. Then let them know what you found useful. That shows respect and builds loyalty.

Make people feel successful, especially in multiethnic groups with status incongruencies. Treat people as adults and as partners. Don't hide behind formal hierarchical position. Earn leadership and respect. It doesn't come with your title.

Spread the glory. When you and your team complete a project, have a recognition luncheon or dinner, and make sure they get bonuses, if appropriate. Don't let yourself be singled out when it was a team effort. You'll generate more support and loyalty, which can benefit you in the future, if you decline to take individual bows.

Your best resource is your staff's ability to generate ideas *and* solve problems. Encourage that. Your job is to create an environment that brings out the best in people. Do that, and it will build loyalty and set you apart from managers who stifle creativity and initiative and diminish intrinsic satisfaction.

Robert Townsend, former CEO of Avis, wrote the book, *Up the Organization* to warn against stultifying management. His follow-up, *Further Up The Organization: How to Stop Management From Stifling People and Strangling Productivity*, emphasizes that leaders should enable people to do a job. He finds most people docile, bored, and dull, and it's their managers' fault. New leaders are often told the people they inherit are the problem, and the solution is to replace them. But good leaders should be able to inspire any group to better performance and solid loyalty. When you face doubts, resistance, disloyalty and noncooperation, Townsend recommends the following:

- Your first impressions are often wrong. Some unimpressive people will turn out to be your best, and some flashy ones will disappoint.
- Some people need security, others need challenge. You need both kinds.

To create a loyal team that will accomplish the goals desired:

- Find ways to compensate for quality work even if bonuses aren't officially available.
- Be fair. Many managers aren't. There's too much injustice.
- Encourage and allow freedom. Allow staff to try and fail, so they'll stretch and achieve more.
- Be discreet. Guard their good name. Handle problems one on one. Don't gossip or belittle your staff in front of third parties.

Don't power-trip. That will undermine loyalty. Don't be a lone ranger, even if you prefer to keep your own counsel. If you're a loner, opponents can organize against you more effectively. So share your thinking and check to be sure you're not missing something. People appreciate being consulted, and by doing so you protect yourself, and strengthen bonds of loyalty.

Don't be secretive, that also destroys loyalty. Old Boys often withhold information. They think this enhances their power, but it actually diminishes loyalty and encourages cliques, distrust, and games. You don't need that, so share information. And help staff try new procedures and innovate. That's easier in a Vanguard culture, but even in an Old Guard company, lead that way. If you communicate to your staff that you trust and respect them, they'll reciprocate loyalty.

Finally, Andrew Grove in *High Output Management*, says:

- Help staff perform better on one important function.
- Help one person on a long-term assignment.
- Get key information for them that will permanently improve their work.

These leverage your own work by helping staff upgrade their performance. Share information on your unit's and the company's overall situation, competitive developments, and production, sales, finances, staffing, and other performance. This gives the big picture and builds loyalty.

Run Meetings Skillfully

Leading from strength depends as much on how well you run meetings as on any other skill. Meetings often are disasters. Plan, prepare for, and think about every meeting. Never wing it. Meetings offer opportunities for sabotage in ways seemingly devoid of racist motives. Don't be a victim. Be conscious of hidden agendas. Choose with care the time, place, attendance, and purpose of meetings you call.

Here are things that commonly go wrong:

- *Confused objectives and expectations.* Know why you called the meeting, and make sure everyone else does.
- *Unclear authority.* Be sure it's the right group to address the issue and that you are in the position to lead it.
- *Avoiding the issue.* Drive for clear definition of problems.
- *Negative vibes.* Make sure the group only includes people who want to be there.
- *Miscommunication.* Listen actively, and see that others also listen. Don't let anyone monopolize.

And before every meeting, check:

- Who will have authority to decide issues?
- What responsibilities belong to whom?

- What type of meeting is it?
- What's my objective in calling it?
- What do I want those attending to do while there?
- How will room arrangements affect what happens?
- Who will follow through on decisions and assignments?

Handle Conflict Thoughtfully

To handle conflicts, get them into the open. You can try to avoid them and hope they'll disappear, but that usually doesn't work. Instead it prolongs hostility and resentment, and the real problems remain. Getting to the real problem may not be easy, because unconscious issues are often at the root. But as far as you can, get assumptions, intentions, fears, and expectations explicitly stated.

To get such candor, build a reputation for being the kind of leader who takes responsibility for your share of problems. And let others see you're trying to see problems from their point of view. Ask for feedback. "Here's how I understand what you're saying. Is that right?" Become known for listening, and you'll be known as a principled leader.

When you reach a tentative agreement, run it by a neutral third party. Then put it in a letter or memo. Be clear on the next agreed steps. You need skill to resolve conflicts that can cause more trouble for you than for most Old Boys and Yammies with wider political support.

Conflicts reveal useful information if you pay attention. So don't look at all conflict as simply negative and undesirable. You can gain insight and improve relationships. Be able to change. After the anger subsides, often both you and your adversaries will have to change or compromise. Don't get personal. And don't try to prove them wrong. Focus on their *point* rather than on *them*.

Keep a Sense of Humor

A leader with a sense of humor can defuse tension and put people at ease. Humor improves communication, motivation, innovation, and output. It helps you adapt to tricky circumstances. It helps improve strained relationships. Humor can help diminish racial issues and reduce the uncertainty and threat you represent.

Don't clown, of course. But easy, natural humor helps create cooperation and respect in uncertain situations. You make people feel comfortable and relaxed with humor. Self-deprecating humor worked for John Kennedy—it can work for you.

Remember, though, that being funny can also be a risk. You can offend. So use good judgment. Avoid ethnic and gender jokes. If you use them, then racial humor would also be okay, and it shouldn't be. The best advice may be to avoid telling jokes in all professional situations. Just notice naturally humorous aspects of daily life, and let the funny moments happen.

Learn to Bargain

Negotiating skills are key to your leadership. Associates may want to test and best you. Their egos require that you can't come out with what you want. Read Roger Fisher and William Ury's *Getting to Yes* and Gerald I. Nierenberg's *The Art of Negotiating*.

Create an atmosphere in which you both hear each other. Often, neither of you has enough power to prevail. So you have to work things out win-win, not win-lose. To lead, you need a good feel for what the other person really wants. Then figure out how you both can get what you want with no one humiliated.

The Modes and How They View Leadership

Mode 1 managers lean toward Theory X, assume most people, including most whites, will subtly resist direction, and adopt a cynical, hard-nosed attitude. They tend toward militaristic, hierarchical postures. They believe fear, reward, and punishment are the basis for respect. They think of themselves as result-oriented.

Mode 2 managers are moderates. They blend participatory and directive approaches, and they compromise more readily. These managers trust and assume good faith responses, but with reservations. They practice Theory Y, but retain control rather than emphasizing participation.

Mode 3 managers assume subordinates want to build a team, can accept interracial leadership, and use a collegial, Theory Z participative style. They assume mutual earned professional respect is the basis for effective leadership.

Mode 1

Henry Clapton

"You're being tested. Whites at any level feel they can test a black at any level. White employees test me managerially, technically, and spiritually. But managers are tested all the time. It's not just race."

Bob York

"Terminate if there's cause, unless the person is truly unaware of inadequacies. I've terminated people I liked. But they weren't doing the job. And they'd had enough counseling. If your superiors honestly tell you what they expect, and you don't get it done, you should be fired. And if people have a different agenda and will not, rather than cannot, do the job, they should be fired."

Stu Elmore

"One staffer didn't like me, didn't like black people, and wanted the job. Every memo he wrote that I had to sign, I read carefully to make sure he didn't hurt me. If I'd signed some, I'd have looked like a jerk. He'd twist facts. I had to catch that. I told him to stop. He said, 'I'll do what I want. You do what you want.' So I split his job, took his field responsibilities away, and left him his central office staff function. Managers reorganize to get around problem people, to take them out of the loop, and take advantage of strengths and weaknesses. Personnel, where he had friends, tried to block me. White people are friends with white people. Two white guys who hate each other will stop fighting long enough to deal with you.

"To handle troublemakers, discipline them in the job's context, not overtly, formally. Reassignment is one good way. Talk and listen, but if there's continuing trouble, wait until it's quiet. Don't threaten and make people defensive. Only act if they can't bring themselves to work with you at all. I promoted the good people. I pulled them closer, talked to them, trusted, used them, rewarded them."

Mode 2

Ben Pringle

"Never let subordinates get around you. That sounds contradictory, I realize, because I found a sponsor by going around my boss to senior management.

"I use three approaches to get subordinates to produce. I let them know what I'm trying to achieve in the quarter. I tell them what their role is, what I think their strength is, how I'm counting on them. We jointly set objectives. After that meeting, they're fired up. Ready to commit.

"The key is, let them know you respect their unique talents, strengths, and capabilities. And make sure they know you recognize their personal qualities. Praise them for good work. I find a particularly good piece of work and ask if they'd mind if I show it to my boss.

"I ask people where they want to go, what's their ambition. Then we help them get a sponsor. That builds loyalty and team spirit and helps protect you, because they appreciate what you've done. So I spend 20 to 30 percent of my time with relationship building. Up and down. My staff gets the work done."

Louise Gibson

"I hit the ground running. I had a knowledge base. So there wasn't a big learning curve. The issue was how to size up the people. In my first line job, in credit, there was a transition. I had three months to come in and leverage my strengths, then take command.

"I ran a process shop and managed client relationships. It was in crisis. There had been problems. We had to cut prices to keep customers. I had to save those relationships. I also had to cut credit losses and tighten collections. But the personnel situation was terrible. People had been badly treated. So we had human resources, product, and system problems. We avoided what had been projected to be $20 million in losses.

"Here I manage strategic planning for product development. How to grow is the issue. We're diversifying. I'm expected to provide a more global perspective. The job needed definition. My boss, who is also black, supports me. And my people brought me up to speed and gave me support.

"In situations like this, I assume there will be roadblocks. But I assume I can make it happen. When I met the chairman, his face showed I was the last person he expected to see making this presentation. He had terrible manners. Another guy also made a presentation, and the chairman turned his back and faced the window. The presenter was undone. If he'd done that to me, I would have said something about it. I don't feel diminutive. I'm only half an inch over five feet tall, but I have chutzpah.

"Jealousy, threat, and competitiveness have come up, but I can't say it was race. I'm good at people management. I spend a lot of time thinking about it and getting a handle on it. That woman over there fired the people she inherited. But I kept mine, and they're loyal. I only hired one person. I walk around. My people know me. And at the lower ranks, that helps.

"They said SVPs never talked to lower-level people. But I coach, train, develop. I'm open to a fault so people know where I'm going so they can support me."

Bill Tompkins

"I've not had much resistance from subordinates. Some people accuse young managers of not digging in and learning the details. But I work hard, and when I make mistakes, I admit them. That wins points with your staff. If you say, 'I didn't do it,' they say, 'That's ridiculous. Why didn't he just admit it?'

"Senior managers will not promote people who are out of favor with their own troops. Managers who see this reality try to be popular. They make popular decisions, but they're often the wrong decisions. They try to avoid flak from the rank and file.

"We promoted a good old boy. He was wrong for the job. Everybody knew it. But they all caved in. Nobody spoke up. So cultivate people. Have them in your corner. Do missionary work all over the organization so you have supporters everywhere.

"When I was first promoted, I was jumped over a lot of managers. There were questions. I was young, black, and didn't have the technical background. Recently, at lunch with a key manager on my staff, he got drunk and said that when I was sent in he was not pleased. 'I had doubts about you. But I'm glad it's working out.' He repeats that story, I'm sure, to others. He's a good man. And that means more, in some ways, than whether I made the numbers in the first quarter."

Carl Wilson

"Take charge. Don't wait when you move to a new position, especially if there were problems you were put there to solve. Start off giving your talks individually and in small groups. Sell your philosophy. Identify and move out the weak people. When the good people see you make commonsense moves they all knew were needed, that's a strong signal you know what you're doing. And it inspires confidence. Don't procrastinate. Implement your plan.

"Make decisions. If you see a procedure or a person won't work out, decide. Race can't matter. Go ahead and manage. I've seen instances where the black manager doesn't get along with the number one producer in the group. But the smart thing, obviously, is to learn to live together. Go the extra mile and make businesslike accommodation.

"You're not there to get along with everybody perfectly. Get beyond the dislikes. Balance toughness with compassion.

"When you recruit team members, you're selling yourself and your organization. If it doesn't work out, ask yourself if you did everything you could to make it work. It's on you maybe more than on white managers to have the skill to make things work. Terminating is hard to do. But I tell my managers they've got to learn to do it and deal with it."

Eldridge Carson, 45, is a production manager in the aerospace industry.

"Blacks have native skills in human relations. We have a natural advantage and sensitivity in personal dealings because of our 'experience.' Some people learn it from a book. We learn from life. I have less hassle with subordinates than do many of my peers. It's not just personality, it's partly culture. We grow up without such clearly demarcated social strata, in general. So we take people as people. But a lot of guys who become leaders in business through class advantage associate business leadership with class privilege and a certain demeanor. And it gets in the way of effective leadership."

Frank Reynolds

"I'm from the South, and we were segregated. In management, I was at first a little intimidated, because my background was, you don't tell white people how to do things. But I don't go into a new environment flexing muscle. Black staffers wonder, 'Who is he? Is he an ally? Is he a savior?' And whites wonder, too. But showing I'm boss is unnecessary. They know I'm the boss.

"I sit with each person and learn their attitudes about what's happening. I find out who are workers and who are complainers. If you flex your muscles, they'll wait for you to stub your toe. And if you wear your rank on your shoulders, that's a mistake.

"Ten years ago, I was an assistant manager in a department that was 95 percent minority and 95 percent female. The manager was white, and most supervisors were white. He came in busting chops—Shape up or ship out. I was a novelty. The women assumed I was there to cry to. They felt they could treat me less than professionally. But I said, 'I'm here to do a job. If you can't hack it, look outside.' It was like I had fifty wives. Some had a professional interest, and some a personal interest, as it turned out. So I was careful. I said, 'I'll work with you and help you solve problems that have been chronic here, but I'll be damned if I'll lose my job for y'all.'

"I went on to become manager. We had a union that helped me solve problems. Working conditions, low pay, and hours were worse than desirable. And we had lots of troublemakers and trouble. One day, we fired ten on the spot. It's too bad we had to go to such lengths, but things turned around.

"In this job, I came in at a senior position. Some people at this bank were concerned, not about whether I would respect them, but about their survival.

"I appreciate the changes necessary. Earlier in my career, I didn't see why people had to clean house. Now I understand. My boss brought me here from our old bank. And I see resistance to him and resentment at changes he's making. But you bring in your own people because loyalty is key. You need people to talk to you about the real issues, not superficial issues. My boss only has to say, 'Frank, get it done.' And he knows it'll get done.

"I'm one of three hundred blacks nationwide at this level. This industry doesn't promote minorities to these positions readily. I have to justify myself, and I'm still being tested. They take the monkey off their backs and put it on mine to see how I handle it. I've had to discipline and terminate middle managers. I had a branch manager who, ironically, was black. He refused to do his job. He had the skills and ability. I had a good relationship with others who worked with him, including his assistant.

"He had a sideline business on company time. His assistant, who was also black, kept me informed. I took account of the fact that she might have been after his job. But, finally, I had to let him go. I asked for his resignation. In this business, it's tough to have been fired. So I didn't want to put a mark, the scarlet letter, on his record. Race *did* influence the decision. I was prejudiced. So I tried to go easy on him. But he continued not to perform, and cost me money."

Joe Wilson

"You have to believe in the Almighty. You can only do so much. You need divine intervention. It helps to have strong faith. I haven't met many atheists in senior management. You have to pray to somebody. More and more, people go back to religion as they move up. And religion is important because of morality and ethics. To lead, you need that.

"People want to know you're competent, fair, and consistent. If you tell them what you want to achieve, and they do it, and you reward them, they'll respond. White folks respond to the dollar. If you help people put money in their pockets, they'll respond to your leadership. So help your people prosper.

"People also look especially to see if you punish fairly those who deserve it. Some blacks bend over backwards to be nice. But subordinates want you to be fair. People know who's not pulling their weight. They want to see justice done. Insubordination is still a good way to hit the street. If they don't respond to directives, policies, and procedures, document it. Put directives in writing if there's a problem with responsiveness. But in the end, I've got to lead.

"If you can logically show why you want to go a certain way, you're entitled to try that strategy. In the beginning, I was challenged on strategy. But follow your judgment. I want to be able to say I did the best I could with the information I had.

"Of course, sabotage can happen. For instance, when I came here, as COO, the sales force sat on their hands, didn't get out and push these new products. They wanted to help me fail. So I changed the compensation plan so if I failed, they failed. I put the branches on a P and L. And I put the salesmen on a plan based on margins and sales so they couldn't just sell with low margins.

"The higher you go, the less people will act against you based just on race, because they, too, will have more at stake. Their standard of living constrains them. They'll think twice before doing something stupid when they're making $75,000 or $100,000 a year."

Al Carswell, 33, is a management consultant with a Big Six accounting firm.

"Know what you're talking about. And be decisive. Make the call, right or wrong. What hurts any manager's credibility is being indecisive. Being indecisive hurts my subordinates. It holds them up. So a bad decision is almost better than no decision."

Alan Roland

"The key to success is building personal loyalty. You're concerned about staff's willingness to work hard for you as well as with their ability.

"Two white fellows worked for me, and this illustrates a common dilemma. One was rough and tumble, a hard drinker. We did not share those values. But when I said, 'George, I've got to get it done,' I could count on him. The other shared my family-centered values. And I could rely on him, too. But I needed the other guy's skills most, the ramrod guy more than the diplomat. The second, I laid off in a downturn. Fortunately, he's still a friend."

Linda Jackson

"Context determines most leadership problems. It's difficult when an older white male reports to you. And it's tough on them when you move into a job and your predecessor has to say to his staff, 'This is my replacement.' It diminishes their status, because it has become a 'ghetto' position."

Carl Cash, 51, worked in human resources management and information systems in electronics firms and state government.

"When I took over, the number two guy set out to orient me. He would convene meetings with me and the people who reported to me. But when he tried to lead the meetings, it was not effective. Then he began to snipe in meetings and became an adversary.

"My boss asked me to take on more and more important projects, and people began to take me seriously. It was awkward. Number two was well connected but was not a factor. He was a dumb liberal, who can be your worst enemy.

"He tried to talk to me about race. He bad-mouthed his former boss, who was black. He knew a lot of blacks but never said anything good about them. I kept my distance. I survived and expanded, but under duress. It was dangerous, with little margin for error. If I made a mistake, they'd be on my case in a minute.

"We were selecting and bringing in a state-of-the-art telephone system. The manager handling that for me was bright. But the project got fouled up on his watch. And he should have been able to straighten it out. But it absorbed a lot of my time. He wanted glory but caved when it got tough. I finally had to let him go. I found out later he had gone to higher management and told them I was incompetent. So watch your back and flanks all the time."

Ossie Gordon

"Most of the people you manage have never been evaluated by a black before. They think they're smarter than you, by definition. So establish that you're boss by demonstrating effectiveness. They have trouble accepting black leadership. This impedes getting quality staff and having them respond.

"Black managers complain they don't have enough authority, but that's the norm. You have to depend on people over whom you don't have formal authority. It's a constraint. So don't worry about formal authority. Just lead."

Art Barlow

"I would take consultants out drinking until two A.M. and then make a meeting at seven A.M. This was, I thought, a way to make them and my staff understand that I was tough and had stamina. And I was testing their stamina. I was competing on every level, including physical stamina. But the younger blacks were trying to establish identity by not being part of the group. They'd distance. You had to ask them to do very specific tasks. They'd do what was asked but didn't initiate.

"Young whites who reported to me were more aggressive. Blacks never challenged, wouldn't question anything I said. But some younger whites challenged all the time. I'd let them do what they wanted. Then they'd get in trouble, and then they'd be willing to listen to me.

"Gradually the younger black consultants became friends with me because they came to see that we needed to protect ourselves mutually, and that I could, in fact, protect them when they did something wrong, as long it was the sort of mistake anyone could make, nothing unusual. But I also had to get across that they shouldn't purposely force conflicts based on nationalistic philosophy. No dashikis. No 'this-is-my-heritage' stuff."

Thelma Morris, 37, is a manager in retailing.

"Too many organizations discourage managers from accelerating your best staffers. I help people move to bigger things. But my boss says, 'Don't do that.' He thinks that's not loyal. Managers transfer losers to others, instead of helping them improve or getting rid of them. That's what leaders should do.

Jim Waters

"When I came here there were no controls or policies. So I put in controls and systems, and listened and watched. Of the staff I inherited, some were loyal to my predecessors, others to the institution. People goofed off. I had to tighten up. I let a black woman go who got a lawyer and charged discrimination.

"Another black woman was strong and aggressive but not tactful. Our major client complained. She had superb writing skills and was talented, first-rate, exemplary, but rubbed people wrong. From one source I'd discounted it. But from many I took it seriously, because it hurt the organization. People suggested things, and she'd reject them. So, on balance, she damaged the program. I finally decided to let her go, and she accepted it. It was painful, because she's very professional. But I couldn't manage around the flaw."

Wes Albright

"An engineer was bright but not competent, had a limited commitment. He gave a good days' work, but I never saw him five minutes past quitting time in seven years. He had lobbied for the job. He'd worked with me at another company years before. He would screw up, then shape up, then do it over again.

"We were growing, and I expected more. So I gave him more work. Then he got closer to my boss, who, like the engineer, was Jewish. And he networked. Other people wrote commendations for work that I knew to be garbage.

"We had sent materials to customers that were rejected. His fault. So I gave him a written warning. But my boss refused to accept it, and so did the human resources department. But by our policy and procedures a manager doesn't need approval to write up a subordinate.

"I was pissed. So I consulted my mentor. He was appalled and offered to go to the head of personnel. He outlined what he saw as my alternatives. I didn't take any. I just let it go. But finally, the guy resigned.

"The biggest problem black managers have is hiring and retaining competent people. A good person who has other options sees working for you as an extra career risk, even if he's a liberal. So you tend to hire mediocre to poor people who have fewer options. So your unit will have poor performance. You'll be criticized. Your reputation will be hurt. And you'll then have even more trouble hiring the kind of people you need to really be effective and successful. It's a vicious cycle."

Lou Benson, 45, is a partner on the tax side of a Big Six firm.

"I've never had a problem with young whites challenging or testing me to see if I know my stuff. But I don't have to do much technical work anymore. That's their job. Three supervisory managers report to me. As it happens, two are black. They do the hands-on technical work. But I keep ahead of them through reading and through experience. I'm in a very technical area. And I was known as a sound technician in taxation coming up in the firm. That's key.

"We hire smart people. And they want you to know it. Some senior people consider a lot of youngsters are pains in the ass, know-it-alls. But I've never had insubordination."

Larry Prince

"I have an easy, informal manner. I treat people the same. I don't make concessions to status, and I respect superiors, peers, and subordinates. I'm VP for finance and administration. I had a controller who had twenty years experience. He had difficulty reporting to me. I was black and younger. Before, he had access to senior management. After that, he had to go through me.

"It came to a head after a year, when I evaluated him. I gave a negative appraisal, the first time in his career. I was excessively harsh to make the point, so we could go forward constructively. But he appealed to the president, who supported me. And after that, we worked out a better relationship. And he improved.

"He had countermanded my instructions, undermining me. So I made the point: 'The next step is out the door if you don't improve. Your work is unsatisfactory. Your experience and knowledge aren't enough. You need to be a team player.' I was prepared for him to quit or, if he hung in and fought, to reorganize around him and let him sit in the corner.

"Another guy, I didn't know if he was trying to undermine me or was just dumb. So I recruited another black Harvard MBA and put him with him. Then I'd only meet with both present. I got my agenda carried out through him. But the guy improved because my new man did the job well, including things the problem person said couldn't be done or would take a long time.

"I needed a black protégé, who was loyal, to help me with my agenda, so I wouldn't have to worry about inevitable racial concerns. And it was a pleasure to have a bright black guy and give him assignments and move him along.

"Oddly, now I'm in a predominantly black company, and I'm sponsoring a white guy, older than me. I recruited him. He's got weaknesses and some discomfort about career prospects in a black company. But I see him as a prospective partner. He's good, but his relationship with me is better than it is with my black partners."

Al Crenshaw

"I'm not a coercive person, not a take-charge-and-order-people-around guy. I'm a consensus manager. I want honest input, so that my decisions are well thought out. But you can't always go for consensus. Sometimes you have to decide alone. You have to lead.

"People are afraid to give me honest viewpoints, to disagree, because they're wary I might go off. Blacks are thought more likely to make a scene. Experience has made me more militant. I've felt subtle discrimination affects my view of situations and people, including other black people. For instance, at a client, I was training users. There was a woman, very quiet, low-key, and very dark. And I thought to myself, 'Boy. She's going to screw up.' But she turned out to be one of the brightest.

"But that attitude that I saw in myself I feel coming against me from whites, including those I manage. So I ask myself, 'Is there a reason people are ignoring me in this meeting? Am I screwing up?' I used to think, yes, it must be me. Now, I'm likely to see the alternative explanation—they behave that way because I'm black."

Bob Mitchell, 51, is a Ph.D. engineer. He's worked in prestigious advanced technical laboratories as an analyst and manager.

"In the lab, I had fourteen master and Ph.D. scientists, including a black computer guy, Cal Tech graduate. He changed jobs every year for five years. That's a danger sign. But I hired him believing it would work. Mistake. He didn't come on time. Left early. Contributed little. I let him go within a year. Very disappointing.

"Two guys tattled on him. I considered them racists. But their reports were accurate. They were hard to manage but told the truth about him. One guy was very good. The other, a Ph.D., was incompetent. I finally demoted him, and he left.

Mode 3

Brad Graham

"People might see me as too easy. I'm not very macho. I set up a teamwork environment to communicate in meetings and one on one. And people who work for me say I'm fair."

Len Crandall, 51, an attorney, teaches at a major law school. He has held senior posts in federal agencies managing lawyers.

"I've gotten appropriate respect because of the credentials. I had taught the subject, knew it thoroughly, and was up to speed quickly. But twice people tried to ignore policy direction. White males are most invested with their own inherent authority.

"One, the head of the appellate unit, was writing a brief. I set a direction, but he told his subordinate that he would do the opposite. I had heard he was assigning blacks on his staff no important work. I had considered him for promotion but began to hear he was a racist. People uniformly reported negatively. So I moved him. And he fought it. We had a hearing, and he lost. Some of his white female subordinates asked me not to bring him back. I moved him to a unit doing nothing, and he resigned. He had flouted my instructions, was arrogant, but bright and competent. I didn't counsel him because it was irremediable.

"In the second case, I asked an attorney to write a brief in a certain direction. He, too, did the opposite and filed the brief. I thought his argument would lose, and it did. I discovered what he'd done, too late. I called him in, and he admitted he'd decided not to follow instructions. He had a legal argument for his decision, a policy rationale. We had discussed the technical issues and, I thought, had ironed out our differences. So I told him I thought his actions inexcusable, insubordinate, and grounds for firing. But I listened to his reasoning and decided he was well motivated. I put a reprimand in his file. He didn't challenge it. In fact, he thanked me for not firing him. Staffers told me they couldn't conceive of him doing that with a white superior. So, in retrospect, it was racial. But at the time, I thought it was just impetuousness.

"Behavior's ambiguous. You can't tell if subordinates are racially motivated or not. It's tough. In the first case, I asked around about his racial attitudes and got adverse comments. But the second guy seemed just overeager. If insubordination isn't limited to a specific situation, a narrow refusal to follow instructions, then it's a general attitude about race, and that's grounds for action. My deputy, who was black, told me how to handle both cases with minimal hassle.

"I asked the second guy, 'What if our roles were reversed, and you were me?' That helped him see how insubordination was serious. I wanted directions followed in the future. But the first guy, who was older, had a character flaw, not just bad judgment.

"I consult with subordinates. I listen carefully to create an atmosphere of collegial, participatory decision making. I like to brainstorm, hear views, ask questions. I phrase my views tentatively. Dialogue actually makes some subordinates uncomfortable, if we treat them as peers. But when they get used to my style, they respond.

"I also had subordinates rate superiors. In law school, students rate us. But my managers were afraid they'd lose control if we tried that. I would have done it anonymously, but they thought people would misuse it and be negative. But I still wanted to see if subordinates were overwhelmingly negative on any managers. And I wanted them to rate me. I thought morale, energy, and diligence was high."

8

Understanding the Value of Loyalty

"My father always told me that all businessmen were sons of bitches, but I never believed it until now."

JOHN KENNEDY

"What would I do without you?"

RAY CHARLES

There are many kinds of loyalty: for instance, gender, management, labor, fraternal, religious, ethnic, regional, patriotic, club, college. All can be sources of pride and create questions of allegiance and strain, on the job and off. But we focus on these six:

- professional, to an overriding ethic and intellectual standard
- personal, to bosses and colleagues
- organizational, to unit and company
- philosophical, to basic values and worldview.
- political, to partisan political causes, parties, and candidates
- racial, to your race's interests and institutions

Which Side Are You On?

In the early 1970s, an executive was asked his evaluation of black managers. He said, "They demonstrate an extremely humanistic outlook. They are keenly aware of the plight of their subordinates, almost too aware sometimes. There seems to be a deep conflict between the managers' relationship to their own communities, and everything that means, and their loyalties to their companies. In the end, these two pulls could take away from their overall effectiveness."

There's a big part of the loyalty issue in a nutshell. That's still how many Old Boys see many African-American managers. They see a clash of values and outlook. The comment illustrates the loyalty issue. Which side are you on? That's what your company's leaders wonder. But it's never put quite that way.

Managing presents difficulties compounded by race. But the profession requires across-the-board commitment from everyone. To lead, know where you stand, what's in your soul. You have a corporate commitment that at times may compete with your other loyalties. Look for loyalty in personal relations, policy, style, partisan politics, and philosophy. Mismatches affect performance.

What You Can Do

With common sense and maturity, you can balance loyalty to your boss, the firm, and your own values and outside interests. But Old Boys and Yammies don't see you as quite fully American. They know you're a citizen, but that's not the same as full visceral compatriotic feeling and shared loyalty.

They think their class and racial interests and the nation's interests are the same. To them, what's good for them is good for the country. They believe people who don't see things from their perspective should participate only minimally. Many give lip service to democracy, but they don't want minority groups with other ideas to have much influence. And you are presumed to want to "social engineer" change.

They wonder how you would use the clout, prestige, and leverage of senior management. How hard would you push for "civil rights?" Will you be a good soldier, do a job for the company, and go home and keep quiet? The answer should be no.

Be professionally loyal. And give personal loyalty to your boss, unless he or she makes it impossible. But social and political objectives should also be important to you. If they're too liberal, you'll pay a price in most Old Guard companies.

Social scientist Mohamed Hussein has a "Third Culture" concept that applies to this issue of loyalty. People increasingly associate across cultures and societies. They work on common projects, and they absorb each other's standards, norms, styles, manner of communicating, and even worldviews. A new "kind of self" emerges. A composite or hybrid person results who transcends the original cultures.

People can simultaneously belong to several cultures. With increased sophistication, they can adopt a cultural identity that fits the circumstances. But even with the interpersonal skills and commonalities that develop from working together, there are still nationalistic loyalties. And these can cause friction, arouse suspicion, and create distance. In any case, you may be perceived as having divided loyalties, even if you are Mode 1 or 2.

Manage Tensions Between Personal and Company Loyalties

The CBS handbook on policy says this: "Because CBS attempts to provide levels of employee compensation which are fully competitive, the company feels entitled to first call on time, energy and output, and the undivided loyalty *in every sense*" of all employees.

In every sense. It's remarkable to see it spelled out like that. But under the racial circumstances in this country that's asking a lot. Surveys purport to show corporate loyalty eroding in general. Managers are tired of shabby treatment. Many now give first loyalty to families and self-interest. Sacrifice for the company is not as important. You're not the only one with lukewarm allegiances. But Vanguard firms still expect and receive high loyalty while racism makes it harder to develop loyalty in Old Guard companies.

The American Management Association also finds loyalty declining. Managers react to mergers and layoffs by withdrawing organizational loyalty, since it isn't sufficiently reciprocated. But the AMA study says many managers still want to be loyal and to be treated loyally. They want to belong and to believe in their employers.

What to do? First, recognize where your personal interests and the company's diverge. Second, understand where they converge. Don't deceive yourself. Some employers appeal to you based on shared values and social purpose. That can earn strong loyalty. But most Old Guard companies can't inspire that kind of loyalty.

If your leaders have vision, that will inspire you and minimize ethnic, racial, class, gender, and other potential sources of disharmony. Well-run companies get everyone focused on agreed goals such as service, quality, innovation, production, sales, and growth. And that builds loyalty.

Don't confuse loyalty to the company with simply "going along" out of a desire for security, risk aversion, or a lack of imagination and creativity. That kind of "loyalty" produces bureaucrats. Ultimately it hurts performance.

Loyalty to the company, its programs, and your associates make sense if you agree with their ends and means and your job is intrinsically rewarding. That's positive loyalty. It's not based on insecurity.

Be True to Yourself

You're probably more liberal than the average Old Boy or Yammie, and most of them prefer to work with people who share their views of how the world should be. That's understandable. But it gives them extra reasons to resist working with you if you want to correct social inequities.

Many see you as more loyal to your race than to the company or the corporate ethic. Further, and with some basis, they see

African Americans as opposed to the corporate and managerial class on some key issues. In the 1960s and 1970s, African Americans often lined up against the Fortune 500 in objection to corporate practices. Picketing over affirmative action, sit-ins over bank lending practices, lawsuits, boycotts, protests over plant closings, and complaints about services and quality in retail and supermarkets were common.

Black people are also seen, and perhaps you see yourself, to some degree as part of the Third World. And the Third World is commonly perceived, even with the emergence of freer markets and more democracy, as statist, non-pluralistic, and hostile to some Western and corporate interests. This perception leads some to associate you with hostile ideologies.

Prominent black leaders have sounded threateningly anticorporate on the six o'clock news, and many Old Boys will associate you with these images, no matter what your personal politics. Furthermore, African Americans have been loyally Democratic and often hostile to Republican candidates and platforms. This, too, puts the black community, and by association you, at odds with corporate leaders and most middle managers. Even Democratic business leaders generally have been moderate to conservative. But many black senior executives and board members have been forces for change beyond the preferences of even liberals on boards or in senior management.

These loyalty factors pose dilemmas for you. You are part of a group with perceived and actual conflicts of interests with your employer. And if you take positions, you identify yourself as one whose policy loyalties are different. These subjects evoke strong reactions, and your adherence to principles can hurt your career. So avoid casual controversy. But don't fly under false colors. Be true to yourself.

Know Where You Stand

Sometimes black and white managers' philosophical differences are based on differing "nationalistic" allegiances. Mode 3s, Bodacious types, make their political and social attitudes known. Their colleagues and superiors understand they have an agenda. But most African-American managers are Mode 2. They're Pressers, occasionally Pushers, and often Lip Servers. They don't openly challenge company policies or aggressively look for opportunities to press for changes.

In years past, Mode 3 conscious change agents who championed racial progress were known as Race Men. That attitude is the philosophy of nationalism. Nationalism comes in many varieties, and most African-American managers, in all modes, are nationalists of some sort, mild to aggressive. Those who are highly nationalistic are incompatible in most Old Guard firms.

You may be in Mode 1, more conservative than most African-American managers. Some black managers who use conservative-sounding rhetoric are cynically opportunistic, in hopes of rewards. But often they don't receive genuine regard, and they risk being seen as insincere and intellectually dishonest. Their Old Boy and Yammie associates—Purgers, Retrogressive, and Ambivalents—pretend camaraderie but suspect them of posturing.

Mode 1 African Americans are often Unconscious; sometimes they are Lip Servers. They risk being seen as untrustworthy by those they seek to cultivate. Some believe what they profess, but Purgers and Retrogressives know there is a conflict of interest.

Perhaps you have no firm views on politics and public policy. You may be a genuinely apolitical Mode 2. That's fine. In any case, the rule is, be intellectually honest and know where you stand. Don't contort logic and self-respect to impress those with whom you have real conflicts. If you have strong views, accept that principled politics will limit your options.

Next to sociability and strong consistent performance, a leading factor determining how far you go and how you'll be rewarded is perceived loyalty. Your corporation is not only interested in economic results. The firm is also a political instrument. Your superiors have to have confidence in your loyalty, and your social outlook, worldview and political philosophy will be important in how loyal you're perceived to be. Perceived disloyalty can block progress. Your boss wants you to protect him, support his agenda, work hard, hit your targets, and be honest. He also wants you to share his worldview and social assumptions. So even if you are in good standing on the team technically and professionally, philosophically you are suspect in many Old Guard companies.

You probably have different opinions on affirmative action, South Africa, minority business support and many social issues. Beyond those questions, you also may have different views on the relative merits of, say, public housing, free market approaches to solving social problems, environmental issues, comparable worth, the Equal Rights Amendment, and so on. There's a good chance you and your boss don't see eye to eye on important public and corporate policy issues. You want different outcomes. But Old Boys expect you to see the world as they do.

In the Reagan and Bush administrations several conspicuous, ambitious African-American administrators expressed strong conservative views. Some gained access and other benefits. (For example, Clarence Thomas gained a seat on the Supreme Court.) Were they respected and valued, or were they used but mistrusted?

It's not just a matter of partisan politics. Regardless of party label, and at national, state, and local levels, in most jobs fitting in has to do with worldview rather than credentials or even race or social background, per se. Black managers don't fully fit, because they want change or are presumed to want change. They are assumed to be liberals. An Old Boy who felt that way wouldn't fit in either. But then, he wouldn't be an Old Boy.

The Modes and How They View Loyalty

Mode 1 managers put loyalty to the company, unit, or boss first. They tend to defer to authority, are comfortable with most corporate traditions, and see little need to challenge unless they are personally victimized. They tend to be politically conservative and are often Republicans.

Mode 2 managers understand the loyalty issue but are pragmatically committed to advance in their careers by playing down differences and diplomatically managing to get along. They are often apolitical.

Mode 3 managers are most likely to defy convention and be outspoken in opposition to prevailing norm. They challenge assumptions and may confront bosses and established procedures over matters of perceived racial group interests. Their loyalties are essentially external, not internal. They are often activist liberal Democrats and are especially mismatched in Old Guard corporations.

Mode 1

Joe Wilson

"In 1988, I voted for Bush on the merits. But I'm independent, and usually vote Democratic. I was approached to get on board early (1989), for Bill Bradley for 1992, but I didn't."

Mode 2

Ben Porter, 50, is an independent consultant and was in international consumer goods marketing.

"Most blacks from elite MBA programs have the same expectations as whites. But they face unique problems. Some wake up and learn that early. But some never do and never succeed. 'Gary Gray,' a white Harvard Business School classmate, can concentrate on his job. The only problem might be personality. But I have to take account of race, too.

"In the seventies, I worked for a big company and was responsible for a region that included Africa. They had a distributor in South Africa and wanted to set up a subsidiary. I went to see the situation. When I met them, I knew we were dealing with a bunch of racist bastards. I came back and said the situation was inherently unstable. We should cut the distributorship back for a few months, then check all angles and decide what to do. The distributor tried to go around me. He went to the president. But I planted doubts about everything he said, and I got the company to change policy.

"Other parts of Africa made more sense for us anyway. At the time, of course, I didn't realize those countries would do so poorly. But you can't make economic decisions divorced from politics. Who you are, your perspective, matters. I could have looked like a loyal team player by just going along. But I wouldn't have felt good looking in the mirror."

Jack Bell

"I'm plateaued, surviving, treading water in a company that doesn't allow people to keep treading. I have to do super, but a lot of people only have to do average. They'll say, 'Let's get him out. He's blocking younger talent.' And they'll criticize and magnify the stereotypes, like being emotional, overreacting, being paranoid and not loyal.

"Blacks are stereotyped as not loyal because they often have to go around managers to get problems resolved. The company doesn't want wild ducks. But it was built by wild ducks, who are actually more like us, when you think about it. And they wonder why they're not growing at the same rate as the competition. We've become bureaucratic like ATT and GE. But I don't let the problems become irreconcilable differences.

"But some of us get arrogant. 'You can't tell me. I know it all.' And some half-step. Let's face it. But be loyal to those you report to, and you'll be successful. Follow orders and don't rock the boat. Cultivate senior support and feed their egos. Tell them what they want to hear, that you admire them. 'How can I be like you?' Build personal loyalty. It's psychological.

"Don't overplay it or seem to just be using a technique, or you're dead. And look out if you opt to fit in and give up independent perspective. Some black VPs have been blasted by other blacks, perceived as sellouts. They paid a price by going along too much with the company agenda."

Bob York

"If you have a controversial opinion on social issues, like affirmative action or South Africa, say so. Just be thoughtful and prudent. If that causes trouble, better to find out early. If you do a good job, you can say what you want."

Alan Roland

"We do business in South Africa. The CEO wanted to expand shipments there. We talked about the business issue, not the politics. Some whites feel guilty about doing business there and get defensive. But here they're comfortable with it, and with me."

Gene Martin, 37, is a Big Six consultant.

"I've been left out of discussions on security issues when associates and superiors didn't really want input. But be objective and professional, and your loyalties seem as solid."

Lon Fellows, 45, is also a Big Six consultant.

"It matters to them that we tend to be liberal. I assumed, working in aerospace, that everyone was right-wing. But actually they saw see me as fairly conservative, except for the 1976 election, when I went for Carter."

Mode 3

Cecil Clemens

"My boss, who hired me, is an active Republican. I told him I worked in Jesse Jackson's campaign. We differ. That's clear. But we talk about it. I'm active in politics, and the partners talk to me about it. They know I'm very liberal.

"A senior partner was a Reagan appointee in California. He invited me to his house. And who's there? Ed Meese. This was a few days after the 'Meese Is a Pig' signs appeared around town. His office is full of Reagan photos. But we get along well. It would not be my politics that would prevent me from getting to senior management.

"Once, at a Stanford black alumni function, a black researcher from the Hoover Institution was at our table. She was to the right of Genghis Khan. But politics don't prevent relationships. Steer away from political discussions. But if you bring in business, you can go to the top. Being a black liberal doesn't block you."

Frank Reynolds

"My old job, at the bank, in community and social lending, was to bring in business. I could commit the bank. But as I increased my efforts, the bank began to decline the loans. I sang these borrowers' praises. The proposals weren't bad. But the criteria were loose and general. So I said, 'You're making it tough and smudging my reputation. When I shake hands, they think it's a deal. Then you turn it down. But you can't say why.' So I concluded the bank wasn't serious. It hurt and pissed me off that after ten years of good reviews I became a liability. I tried to shrug it off.

"Then my boss left and came to this bank, and I had the chance to follow. He's given me respect and opportunities. I feel comfortable, like a partner. I want them to feel I helped build this bank. But I learned hard lessons. Policy differences are dangerous, especially if there's a political and philosophical dimension."

Brad Graham

"It's difficult to know if whites are racially motivated or are simply practicing favoritism and cronyism. They resist competent blacks and those who are outspoken on racial matters."

Ben Allison

"I've had conflicts with peers, but I talk it out, try to make him comfortable. Kid and visit with him. The problem is usually ignorance. So I try to let him know me, and it works out. I try not to threaten. But my worldviews and values are different. The company realizes it needs heterogeneity, so they get people with points of view like mine. But there's a thin line between acceptable perspectives and those that threaten.

"My manager and I talk about anything. And I'm lucky he counsels me on how to handle company politics. Value conflicts are most important but difficult to resolve. You have few choices. You can say, 'Look. This is how you feel and think, and how I feel and think. Let's deal with that.' But if you let people see who you really are and they don't like you, you're finished. You can withdraw or find a situation where your values and the organization's are in sync.

"Take Africa, for example. Those nations are important to the future of our business, and the world in general. But in high tech, where I operate, they're uninteresting, with a few exceptions. No marketing opportunities yet. In narrow business terms, we won't sell many units in the next ten years. But Africa is important for other reasons. So my view is different. It's not just identification with my people. Some may become customers. So, for business reasons, it's shortsighted to be merely a Europhile. I see things they don't."

Carla Peters, 50, is a corporate lawyer and a Republican.

"If they attack my dignity, I'll walk. I can live on less income without worry. The things I want in life aren't expensive. Whites think you want to be with them. But the people I like most are blacks. I wasn't panting after what they had. And that attitude offends them. I don't find them valuable or interesting, so I don't try to get close. I need a good blanket, a reading lamp, and some good books. The company isn't a source of a rich life, just a paycheck. I keep my life separate. But most blacks try to blend work and social life."

Ralph Adams

"I was outspoken, supported liberal candidates, and had political posters in my office. My boss was an old army guy, crew-cut. His boss was a right-wing southerner and a religious fundamentalist. They were suspicious of me. They thought I was associated with the outside critics of the firm. I had been critical and not loyal. I organized a petition among the black professionals, twenty-five of us out of fifteen hundred in the firm. We asked for changes in consulting policy and personnel practices. That was seen as hostile, threatening, and disloyal."

Ward Hampton, 55, works in the Washington office of a major manufacturer as a lobbyist. He has worked in politics and run for office.

"In my job, it doesn't matter whether you're conservative or liberal. We discuss technical and political issues despite personal feelings. In government relations, you have to be able to do that. It's easier with commonality. But it's not impossible to work with ideological opposites."

9

Negotiating the Minefield of Office Politics

"Come now, let us reason together."

LYNDON JOHNSON

"Anything you can do, I can do better."

IRVING BERLIN

"Don't let the green grass fool ya."

WILSON PICKETT

"I heard it through the grapevine."

MARVIN GAYE

The business world is increasingly organizing around the flow of information rather than around geography or products. The new business structure, as Peter Drucker observes, may not look so different from conventional structures, but managers will behave differently because different emphases will drive decisions. Organizations will be flatter. Fewer managers will process and package information on its way up. More will produce—make, sell, finance. Fewer will study and coordinate.

Leadership will depend, in these new circumstances, less on political skill and cronyism, especially as Old Boys are weeded out. So you will have a better chance to be effective and fairly evaluated. Drucker uses the metaphor of the orchestra for the new corporate configuration. Pay attention to the "score" as it evolves, and perform as a member of the ensemble.

Management by objectives—and by mature, professional, self-starting and self-controlled managers—will be the mode. But promotions may be more problematic. Integrity, candor, and honesty will be highly valued. Gamesmanship will be less so.

Office politics includes practices like:

- playing hardball
- interpreting the SOP and rules and regulations narrowly, when there could be a more liberal interpretation
- whispering to besmirch another's reputation and credibility
- rumormongering
- backstabbing, usually by privately recommending adverse actions against someone who would expect support—or at least neutrality
- willful lying
- double-dealing and treachery

Other related damaging practices include:

- taking credit for others' ideas
- stealing ideas and running with them
- character and reputation assassination

You become a political target because of:

- too rapid a rise
- personality differences
- too much reward
- disagreements that have become personal
- some transgression you've committed or some slight, disrespect, or offense you've given, whether intentionally or innocently

That's what we mean by office politics—a dangerous game in which a lot of political objectives are accomplished by damaging reputations. To protect yourself:

- Concentrate on your craft, quality, leadership, and self-awareness.
- Add real value—make a consistent positive contribution.
- Produce results that please your boss.
- Cultivate friends in high places who can vouch for your good name.

What You Can Do

Protect Yourself on Paper

Acknowledge the realities of your office politics. Many managers hate the games and injustices. Adversaries are reassigned, reorganized, downgraded. Contracts are shifted. Sometimes there's a solid business reason. But often there isn't, especially when decisions are based on shifting power, personal vendettas, and score settling. But whoever is out to get you is also vulnerable. And there are people who want to get them.

These are common political experiences:

- A colleague turns hostile in a meeting and attacks your proposal.
- A trusted subordinate goes to your boss with opinions that undermine you.
- Your project succeeds, but your boss takes the credit.
- A task force is formed to study your unit, but you're not told in advance.
- You're not informed about coming budget cuts.
- There's a reorganization, and you'll have less access to senior managers.

These common political problems can be compounded by race and made harder to counter effectively in Old Guard companies. Don't be paranoid, but don't be naive. Some colleagues who seem friendly will sacrifice you for their interests. So *document your actions with letters, memos, and copies.* And give "notice" to potential adversaries when your situation requires a paper trail for a possible later confrontation. It's unfortunate, but you may have to be bureaucratic. People will challenge your credibility. So, *protect yourself with paper*. It's insurance against lies and treachery.

Don't Get Isolated

If senior managers put you in a slot, but middle managers object, they may try to keep you out of the loop, a common political tactic. Even though you get along with them and feel accepted and respected, you can still be sidestepped. So concentrate on superior performance. That makes it harder to isolate you.

You still depend on Old Boys and Yammies for help and cooperation. Some were rivals, and perhaps still are, even if they report to you now. So let them talk out their feelings. That can help them accept the realities and minimize the political backlash.

Don't Waste Energy on Payback

Much office politics is about getting even—revenge and retribution. Don't fall into that. Don't bear grudges. Don't fantasize about getting even. Save your energy for productive work, because success is the best revenge.

The ostensible winners, in the short term, often get theirs in the end. Office politics is dangerous. The Yammies and Old Boys who play Machiavelli are often crude and clumsy. They leave footprints and fingerprints. Payback can be rich. All you have to do, often, is bide your time. Your enemies will hang *themselves* eventually.

John Kenneth Galbraith was not fond of Richard Nixon. Galbraith predicted that Nixon would find a way to accomplish a difficult, if not impossible, trick: he would eventually "pick himself up by the scruff of his own neck, and toss himself out on his own ass, into the street." And so he did.

Understand the Environment

Allan Kennedy and Terrence Deal's *Corporate Cultures* offers four ways to see organizations:

1. *Macho Tough Guy*—Construction, advertising, cosmetics, entertainment. High pressure and high financial stakes. Intense competition among coworkers, tricky politics, and frequent blood.

2. *Process*—Insurance, utilities, and government. Bureaucratic emphasis on process rather than results. Many poorly led, unproductive meetings.

3. *Bet Your Company*—Natural resources, mining, petroleum, architecture. High-risk investments in projects with long-term paybacks.

4. *Work Hard/Play Hard*—Computers, real estate, high tech, direct sales. Customer satisfaction is the driving concern. Collegial work relations, with informality and hands-on leadership.

How do you match in personality, objectives, and preferred management style? You may find the toughest office politics in Process and Bet Your Company environments. That's where cultural conservatism will be strongest.

Be a Team Player

Team play is praised. But often that phrase really means "Go along with the group on this bad decision. Don't question the leader's competence. And don't question the holes in the logic." Old Boys like that kind of team play because it protects them. Independent thinking threatens. They want you to go along so the leader's incompetence won't be shown up.

What do you do? Don't gratuitously rock the boat, but don't abdicate your own best judgment. Sound technical and independent thinking will raise issues that need to be on the table. Unless there's a disaster ahead, make your point. Then the debate is over. Help accomplish the project goal, despite defects in management's approach.

To Get Along, Go Along

Sam Rayburn advised Lyndon Johnson that this was how to make it in Congress. Differences of opinion can lead to confrontation. You reach a point where, on principle or on practical grounds, you need to take a stand. But ask yourself how much of the conflict is egos clashing and how much is based on substantive differences.

Race gives confrontation an extra charge, as does other status incongruence between adversaries. Unless facts and political leverage are on your side, let confrontation pass. If you're concerned about a course of action, speak up early before the issue becomes politicized—get on the record. After that, be careful. You've done your professional best.

Grin and Bear It

Closely related to "Let it pass" and "To get along, go along" is "Grin and bear it." To survive in a political environment, use all three approaches.

Grin and bear it means recognize that a course of action or an organizational practice makes no sense, but you can't let on you're disturbed about it. This approach has to be rare, reserved for instances where to survive, you can't even object.

Be Careful About Loose Talk

Henry Rosofsky, former dean of Harvard's Faculty of Arts and Letters, says he was advised when he took the job to "listen to gossip." Obviously, be plugged into the grapevine to get early warning of news that might affect you. But there's a price for that benefit. What reciprocity is expected or required? Whom do you have to interact with to get the word early? In many companies, the plugged-in people are not the kind you want to be close to or identified with. Some are more fascinated by politics than by performance.

Be Honorable and Tell The Truth

To avoid creating enemies, be honorable in all dealings and be consistently principled. Not all managers play it straight. Personal, professional, and technical integrity makes your life relatively free of politically motivated opponents. Let it be known that your word is good, you're consistently loyal, and you don't switch sides for short-term advantage. Build that reputation, and then schemers will have trouble enlisting any cooperation against you because there'll be few you've offended.

A New York Times/CBS poll found only 32 percent of Americans think executives are honest, while 55 percent think most aren't. But only 18 percent of black people think business leaders honest. That probably reflects the real-life experience of most African Americans in dealings with corporations as employees, customers, and citizens. Black managers, likewise, also seem to believe that many, and perhaps most, of their associates cut corners and are dishonest wheeler-dealers. In Old Guard companies, it tends toward survival of the fittest. But it's not quite that way, fortunately, in Vanguard companies.

Be an honest broker. Give your candid opinion, and you can develop a reputation that protects from drifting into trouble. On the other hand, don't try to be the soul or conscience of the company. People resent that. They'll snipe at you, because they'll sense you think you're more virtuous than they, and will try to show you aren't so noble. Tell the truth diplomatically and keep an open mind.

You may be talked about if you're trying to change anything. If in any way you don't conform, opponents will try to diminish your good name. "We've been 'buked and we've been scorned. We've been talked about sure as you're born." The old hymn and anthem of the civil rights movement and the Mississippi Summer Project of 1964 also applies to office politics. You'll be talked about, however competent you are, if you take a contrary stand on substantive issues.

That includes expressing differences on external issues that are at odds with overarching Old Boy social agendas. Opposition on these matters marks you, even if you avoid job-related differences. Your political problems are compounded if your social conscience moves you to act against injustices. So take care in discussing public issues, or company problems that are social or political. Many office political problems arise for African Americans because they're seen as out of step.

James E. Challenger, president of the outplacement firm Challenger, Gray and Christmas, suggests you try to remain popular. Allowing yourself to become disliked by someone in authority "is the single most important reason why people are discharged, not their lack of skills and abilities." So don't talk to anyone who wants to criticize your boss. Even if you just listen, you're implicated.

And don't assert on anything controversial unless it's relevant to your job. Take positions contrary to your superior's carefully, and only directly. Don't complain offhand around the water cooler to some third party.

Managers send and receive information. You represent your unit to others. Any restrictions, political or otherwise, limit your effectiveness. So a common political ploy is to distort or misquote information. If you feel access is restricted, talk to your boss and get outside perspectives. Do that with any political problem: isolation, gossip, retaliation, or circumvention.

Don't Sweat the Small Things

The French say that living well is the best revenge. Remember that. Don't get mad. Instead, achieve and keep your eye on your objectives. Never mind the political games. Concentrate on projects and programs you've created that matter to you and that you can take credit for. That will allow you to ignore petty politics. The best response to those who malign or attack you, or try to circumvent or exclude you, is to excel at these tasks.

When you've been wronged, bide your time. Don't react. Check with your friends and think through your response. The right move is usually simply to let it pass. But when you need to respond, do it rationally rather than angrily.

Black managers aren't uniquely harassed or vulnerable. Many managers feel disappointment and stress. Yammies and Old Boys, and even Stars, have plenty to complain about. But the smart ones focus on the task. If you feel abused and unappreciated, put it in perspective. Your associates endure organizational slights and injustices, too. Unless you're a born diplomat or a born Machiavelli, you'll come up short sometime in a political tussle.

Effective politics depends on your tangible value added. You can only politic after you've established that you're worth having on the team and that you contribute to the bottom line. Adding value is the best politics. Blend into the corporate ensemble. Concentrate on that. If you're a valued member of the team, and the Solids and Stars know it, it'll be tougher for the Yammies and Old Boys to hurt you.

The Modes and How They View Office Politics

Mode 1 managers, assuming most colleagues will act in bad faith, believe deeply in developing and using political skills of all kinds. They see organizations as dangerous and associates as potential aggressors. So they adopt a hard pragmatic view that it's dog eat dog. Ethical considerations are generally set aside in the belief that when in Rome, do as the Romans do. They seem to enjoy the process and function well in most bureaucracies and Old Guard situations.

Mode 2 managers assume most colleagues will act in good faith but, as a practical matter, are ready for anything. They can initiate hostile maneuvers if they see a clear payoff, but they're reluctant to do dirt, and they don't relish the practices. They're better off in Vanguard settings.

Mode 3 managers are almost purists about staying above the fray. They believe the work should speak for itself, and they'll seldom look for a political opening to get to an objective. They have a strong ethical aversion to using any Machiavellian tactics, and they disapprove of those who do. They function best in strict meritocratic settings.

Mode 1

Earl Newsome

"People have tried to go around me. I was thirty-five. I had thirty subordinates. Most were older. They assumed, at first, that I was not fully qualified. But I wrote notes on many issues that conveyed a thorough grasp of the substance.

"Do that. Quickly get past peoples' doubts when you enter a new situation as a leader. Establish that you belong, that you're right for the job, and earn respect. That reduces the political games, end runs, and so on.

"But one guy had a reputation for abusing secretaries. I can't stand abuse in hierarchies. People don't have to take guff. His secretary said to me, 'I have to take time off for personal reasons. But I don't want to tell him. So I'll tell you.' She then came in on her day off. He was ranting and raving. And he was going to dock her. I said, 'What's this? We're human beings.' He said, 'I don't like your attitude.' I got up from the desk and said, 'What the ____ do you mean, you don't like my attitude?' We argued. Then I wrote a note to the file to cover the circumstances, laying out why I handled it the way I had. He then worked an end run. He got himself taken out from under me and got independent authority. I should have mashed him. It was gross insubordination.

"I also had a guy who thought he was safe. He thought more of himself than I did. He was not stupid, but he was pedantic. He was working on a memo, and I told him how I wanted it done, but he did it his way. So I wrote him a note saying that after we talk about a controversial issue, I expect it done my way. I said, 'I won't tolerate that.' And I looked him dead in the eye. We had no further problems. The key is direct, firm, clear communication with people who test your authority, end run, or otherwise disregard your decisions.

"Some younger blacks don't realize it's a hardball game. They think they're still at their mother's breast. They're in another world. They think the environment will be indulgent. It won't."

Carl Wilson

"People look out for their own. A black guy complained that his new boss brought his right-hand man with him. I said he was just looking out for him. That's not racism. White people don't think about you in situations like that. Results count in the end, no matter what else goes down."

Bart Watson, 52, is a senior executive in an office equipment company.

"We have to be guerrilla soldiers to survive. In this, we have to be 'better' than the average limited bureaucrat. Corporations are political. Make alliances. Be skeptical of what you hear. Watch the interactions."

Mode 2

Mel Wilson, 54, is a university administrator.

"Office politics comes with the territory. It's part of life. I don't know any organization that's not political. So get familiar with the ground rules and comfortable with the game. New-comers are at a disadvantage. But develop a healthy attitude about the politics. People try to keep or gain advantages by using old networks. Blacks are hurt if they simply see that as grossly unfair. Just accept it."

Cecil Clemens

"We might be the object of political campaigns more than others. Your authority might be challenged more. You know, 'Shouldn't we check first with the senior manager?' That's politics. Or your instructions or requests aren't responded to as quickly or completely. But everybody has input on decisions in teams. And that allows people to question your authority legitimately, if you want to look at it that way.

"I managed a big project. I had several of the firm's partners on the team working for me. I had to pull in resources from all over the country. I had full authority to kick ass and take names. Rarely did anyone go around me to the managing partner or to the partner in charge. I resolved matters. I'm a strong manager, fairly formal, decisive. I'd say, 'We can't keep debating the issues.' And I was backed up.

"My decisions are always subject to upper management review. So if anyone doesn't like my decision, he can ask for review. That's no problem. I can defend my judgments. But whites don't challenge me unduly. Anyhow, I can't be concerned about people going over me. 'If you want to go higher, fine. But I've got to keep moving.' Some people probably feel I'll run over them. And I will. If I'm given the job to do, I do it."

Len Crandall

"I don't see much office politics. But I do see black staffers do the basic work, develop the case, then the director hands the case to a senior white who gets the glory.

"People of good character, trustworthy, not voracious and greedy, well meaning, don't succeed that well here. We don't fight for position here. We are strongly committed to the overarching objectives. Feathering our own nest isn't the issue it is at some places. Of course, there are some glory hounds who want lots of recognition. But if the project requires teamwork, you can't have much politics."

Harry Nelson, 53, is a senior manager in a U.S. government regulatory agency.

"You won't get a job here on the merits. Assignments are political. It's not fair or valid. I came here to direct a new Office of Consumer Response and to handle information systems and automation. But the senior people were computerphobic and slow introducing systems.

"Automation slowly caught on, and volume picked up. Keeping track of activity became a major problem. The director said, 'We've got to get on top of this. I want you to move to field operations. The problem is, we have limited slots at your level. So we have to ask you, temporarily, to drop two grades.' It was a ploy to nail me. You have to have paid your dues. And they really don't want blacks at senior levels anyhow. So I said, 'No thanks.' But they tried to muscle me into the assignment. I said, 'You can try whatever you want. But you better do it by the rules.' They said my unit was underperforming, and I was vulnerable. That was b.s. But I hung in there. So now I'm on their list. They tried to force me out but failed.

"I came from outside at a high level. These guys worked their way up. So that's a factor. It's not just race. They feel if they plateau me and wait long enough, I'll leave. It's not a hostile environment. I get along with all the whites who actually hate each other's guts. But they can't nail me on qualifications. A former chairman brought me in. But there have been two since then. Senior people wanted to get me and thought they saw their chance.

"The corporation wanted a new approach with our clients, and I was perceived as committed to the old chairman's approach and still loyal to that regime. So my loyalty to current policy is in doubt. I'm not out of sync with current philosophy at all. But I can't convince them.

"My latest evaluation says, 'Independent. He seems to crave responsibility.' It's like, 'What's the matter with this guy?' I teach at the university, and I'm active in the community. Hope springs eternal. The board and the chairman will change. I'll be reinvigorated. I lost a mentor and made enemies but decided to ride it out until the climate changes. That's just a political reality."

Art Barlow

"Here, the idea is to make you look dumb. They'll give the same assignment to three different people. They think of it as constructive competition. But the way it often turns out, the winner is the guy who kills the other two. In this environment,

I often feel people are out to get me. To survive, I make myself clear in all communications.

"People try to steal my better staff members, who're always getting calls to join to some other unit. That's a popular form of politics. Weaken the other guy by stealing his top producers. But, unfortunately, my staff is loyal. I'd be embarrassed to steal staff. But my colleagues do it all the time. It's the shark theory—if you show blood, you're eaten.

"I have a high quota to reach. Once, I had a bad year. And in a meeting, a guy said, 'We're having trouble in this division because Art let us down.' That kind of attack is a good way to zap someone.

"Since I'm light-skinned, I've had people say I have more white blood than black blood, and that's why I'm successful. That's how they make themselves comfortable when I outperform them."

Bill Farley, 47, is a senior officer in a Philadelphia bank.

"If you're promoted based on performance, your peers' respect will be based on your abilities. But if it's not clear why you're selected, you can have trouble getting cooperation. So do some missionary work. Stress that it's a partnership, in the company's interests. And stress that they'll personally benefit from good performance."

Stu Elmore

"Once, some staffers went around me. I found out and quietly adjusted how I dealt with them. No confrontation. I told one guy not to end run. But I react quietly. Learning it was happening was important. You have to be able to find that out. Same with rumors. Let them go. Rumormongers sooner or later discredit themselves with false ones. Just be sure to have someone tell your side. The fire chief doesn't put out the fire himself.

"Reach out. Go touch bases. Diplomacy is important. Don't become self-important, because if you think people *have* to come to you, you lose, sooner or later."

Brad Graham

"When I came into this accounting firm, I negotiated a salary that was almost the same as some seniors'. It rubbed some the wrong way. I worked hard on a proposal for one of them. Then it got back to me that he said it was the worst thing he'd ever seen. He then did an all-nighter, rewrote it, and it was on my desk the next day. But word processing had scheduling problems. And we got the proposal to the client late. This guy had tried to make me look bad and himself like a hero. There wasn't anything terribly wrong with my draft. I knew then that I had to watch him. But to be professional, you mitigate the anger that arises in office politics."

Jack Bolter, 50, was a manager in a large consumer electronics company.

"I was unable to be diplomatic. Situations were always win-lose. To get quality results, black managers have to take charge. But this can cause problems. If you're just a team member, others will get most of the credit. But if you quarterback the effort, then you get your due. The problem is, if you take charge, you're 'overaggressive'—so it's no-win."

Mode 3

Bruce Thatcher, 32, is with a major communications company in marketing.

"When your boss is not performing, who do you tell? You can't tell his boss. So you have to help it show up and hope others notice. And that, too, is politics.

"To deal with opponents, challenge people publicly in meetings. If they have hurt your work, open them up, diplomatically, to scrutiny. Point out their inconsistencies in front of others.

Make them defend themselves. But be sure you have your act together, because they'll challenge you in return.

"There are lots of potential game situations. But I'm here earlier, stay later, and work more weekends than almost anyone. That's how you defeat political games. No matter how silly or demeaning a task, I do it perfectly.

"We brought a hundred people to the Inaugural Ball in 1988. A great success. We brought in our best clients. And we got our CEO to meet them. That was impressive. But it took a lot of work to bring it off. And I got a huge bonus, on top of my regular bonus. They noticed. Believe it.

"Two years ago, I went to New York every week to open a new office. I was determined that it would be smooth. Nobody else would have done that. But the personal sacrifice was overwhelming. When it was over, I gained respect and credibility. And that made it tougher for anyone to do me in. I develop extra insurance against political snipers by overperforming. It's not fair, but that's the way it is. I outwork my enemies. Sometimes they win. But in wins and losses, I'm ahead.

"This firm is lean, and I'm visible. I can call the president. We're a $500 million company, but we work smaller. In a larger bureaucratic organization it would be more difficult to do some things I do. I've moved fast and been shot at. But it's cyclical. Sometimes people are after me, and sometimes they lay off. But my track record is solid. I've proved myself. So they have to back off a lot more. If I were promoted again soon, I'd get more heat. I'm only thirty-two, and I've been here eight years. But the next step would raise eyebrows. So I have to wait two to three years."

Ben Allison

"My conflicts are with peers. I talk it out. I try to make them comfortable. I go out of my way to joke and visit. It's usually ignorance. One guy who didn't know me made statements. So I let him know me better. And we turned out to be likable people. But if the problems were based on title, level, background, it wouldn't have been as easy to fix. In that case, you try to live with it."

Karen Hopkins, 38, is a manager in banking.

"I avoid fights. Let others fight. I have no enemies. I may choose sides, but I don't get sucked in. I don't comment on gossip. People try to feel you out and get you on their side. Avoid that."

Adele Belmont

"There's little you can do to protect yourself from office politics. We're vulnerable. The senior VP wanted my boss to hire a friend, but my boss hired me. So the SVP hired his buddy anyhow and put him over me. My boss, who is also a black VP, resents it. The SVP could have put the guy in another department. But he figured my boss couldn't stop it."

Larry Prince

"They tried to isolate me. I'm weak politically. I don't make the effort to form alliances. I believe merit and good work will get you rewards. But it doesn't really work that way. You have to build alliances.

"With me, if it happens spontaneously, okay. The links should form naturally. But realistically, I'll need relationships based on friendship, not just on performance. Being naive about alliance building is dangerous. I should have built a better relationship with the boss. We had respect. But there came a point when she, in her escalating paranoia, began to see me as in the enemy camp. She saw people as with her or against her. I tried advice. But she didn't listen. Now I see that she was influenced by some of my old enemies, who got to her and warned her against me."

Ted Weaver

"I would have had to play games and do the politics if I'd stayed in personnel at the airlines. There are a lot of cheaters and connivers who have to find out who's on their team. To get ahead, they cheat on their bosses. Most people in business cut corners.

"Contractors pad contracts. Lots of managers screw their customers to make the bottom line come out. We've lost all sense of fair play. Managers don't come out and say, 'Do this or that,' but you get the message. But blacks, generally, aren't in that loop at the level where you have to play that game. Some political games involve winking at stuff, going under the table. You'll have to fit the culture. And cheating is part of it.

"You can read people. I was just in Chicago talking to the chairman of a major financial firm. He said, 'There are more crooks than ethical people in business. More are cheating than not.' "

Al Carswell

"I try not to get involved. I'm not adept. But I don't know if I should be proud of that. That's a big part of what happens here. It's a highly personal environment. Getting resources, assignments, people, salary, projects—it all requires political skill.

"I have a squeaky-clean reputation. But to get the goodies, play politics. Take partners to lunch. And speak out more. But I'm doing the Lord's work, something tangible, useful, lasting. That satisfaction is more important than playing games."

Gene Martin

"I ignore rumors and stay above the rumor mill. I hear a lot, but I stay out of it. No loose conversation. Blacks talk more among ourselves than we tell our white colleagues. But I'm careful. If you say something, it will be twisted. And sooner or later, someone you didn't want to hear it will. Keep confidences, and keep a reputation for integrity. It's not easy for us to relate anyway. So be known as discreet. Don't pass on rumors or listen to whispers."

10

Socializing
With Colleagues

"Some enchanted evening, you may see a stranger, across a
crowded room."

OSCAR HAMMERSTEIN II

"Personal beauty is a greater recommendation than any letter
of introduction."

ARISTOTLE

"He has spent his life best who has enjoyed it most."

SAMUEL BUTLER

"Stir it up."

BOB MARLEY

Do you socialize with colleagues? How often? Where? And is it
artificial, an obligation, or a quality experience? You can relax and
enjoy the experience, but it can also pose problems that require
extra effort. You have little room for error. Even if your company's
culture is permissive and laid back, be careful and conservative. If
there's a misunderstanding or unfortunate incident, it can cost you
more than it would others.

What You Can Do

Don't Overrate It

Socializing is part of your job. You may lack some social opportunities, but it's not that big a handicap. Being self-aware and committed to quality makes up for most social disadvantages. Actually, most managers feel socially excluded, more or less. There's less social contact than you might imagine. The sense of social disadvantage based on race is largely an illusion.

Contact and friendship at church, club, and in colleagues' homes is fine if it's natural. But where there's ambivalence, it can feel unnatural. Not long ago all clubs were exclusive, but restrictions have loosened. So now ask yourself, "Do I want to join?" And why? These settings can be awkward. Coworkers can make careless remarks, tasteless jokes, or ignorant gestures. Miss Manners would not be amused.

Louis Harris did a survey for *Newsweek*. It found that executives' spouses (read, wives) considerably influence business decisions. And their wives are less conservative than they are. Twenty-five percent of senior executives say wives influence decisions on selection and promotion of subordinates. What happens at company social occasions can be significant. So how you handle yourself around the boss's wife matters.

The poll also found that 45 percent of executives said their wife's influence was significant on the policy of hiring minorities. This fits the stereotype of the liberal wife of the crusty dinosaur. But it's suspect, since it probably flatters respondents to say they have socially conscious wives. They gave the expected answers, so the results may be meaningless. In any event, how you conduct yourself and come across is important. So polish your performance.

If You Date at Work, Be Rational

Leslie Westoff's *Corporate Romance* examines the inevitable sexual attraction on the job. She says romance won't work when one reports to the other. That creates problems for everyone, directly and indirectly involved.

Don't let relationships compromise professional relations. Don't date where it might appear you're sharing sensitive information unfairly, to other people's disadvantage. It's okay to date someone in a parallel function, or in a different product area, and as long as you don't have the same boss. But don't flaunt it. And some experts recommend you don't get involved at work—simple as that. It's a big world. Find who and what you need elsewhere. Of course, you can get to know someone in eight to twelve hours a day. You can connect. Just don't let it happen. Why complicate life?

Eliza Collins, in a *Harvard Business Review* article, says managers in love cause dysfunction and harm the organization. The pair creates a coalition. This threatens others, who worry about being excluded from information. Subordinates worry you might be unfair to them and show favoritism. And senior managers worry they might have to intervene at some point. Why precipitate problems? Other observers, like Rosabeth Moss Kanter, say don't worry unless you're indiscreet. She believes we should understand and support people in any personal issues—with children, divorce, drugs, alcohol, illness, mid-life crisis, or when they're in love.

But you're black. Whether your human impulses would be as readily understood and supported is open to question. And you don't need more questions. There are enough uncertainties about matters of direct importance to your performance and effectiveness. Don't introduce wild cards that are discretionary. But if you can't help yourself, you're a human being first. Just remember, there's a double standard.

The Modes and How They View Socializing

Mode 1 managers say socializing with associates, colleagues, and customers is a natural, effortless part of the manager's job.

Race poses no special barrier, and there's little or no exclusion or disadvantage.

Mode 2 managers say socializing requires a special effort and can be awkward or even risky. It's a mixed blessing—being included is important, but they'd prefer to bypass some activities.

Mode 3 managers say socializing poses real risks or is quite exclusionary, and the barriers to entry interfere with full functioning on the job. They find socializing a serious impediment and so problematic that they sometimes see it as an extension of work rather than a true form of recreation and relaxation. For them, it's something to avoid as often as not, and it's too often not worth the effort.

Mode 1

Cecil Clemens

"Here, it's strongly urged that you wine and dine clients. It's a big part of the job. Every year we have a major golf and tennis outing. And you're always free to take clients to play golf or tennis. I'm thinking of learning golf because it's key at upper levels. I've been invited, and I should go. Blacks have a social disadvantage, but we can overcome it.

"The partner I report to didn't hire me. Her boss did. And I'm social with him and with other partners. I've had managers, not partners, to my house. You've got to have an easy personality, get along with colleagues. If you don't, you won't go far.

"They can buy talent up the wazoo. But they need people who can relate. That's the most valued talent in business. Blacks who are loners or lack self-confidence don't make it. One guy never went to lunch with white colleagues. One day, he overheard his boss making a racial slight about him. He asked me what to do. I said, 'Raise it with the partner in charge.' He did. Later, his boss apologized. But bad feelings remained. He couldn't relate to that supervisor. His reviews were low, and eventually he left. But he lacked communication skills and personality for this environment."

Lou Benson

"Younger blacks and whites work easily together. My subordinate managers are best friends. They go to lunch, socialize, and help each other. Two are moving on up together—both are bright as hell.

"All over the firm there's lot's of informal socializing across racial lines. Stories about racism resurging exaggerate. Things are improving. Of course there's racism. But there was more in the 1970s. The climate is better, despite what we read about how Reagan made things worse.

"We have a lot of jocks in this firm. I was a pretty good athlete, too. And we used to win the CPA league title all the time. Now these guys are partners. And I continue good relationships with them.

"There's exclusion from country clubs and city clubs. A friend, a partner in another firm, Yale, Harvard MBA, was turned down for a leading country club. I was set to join a club. But when he told me that, I said, 'To hell with it.' He was really pissed. It matters. We use these clubs. The firm pays. Why should I help pay others' memberships, indirectly, if I can't join myself? Some are for bluebloods. If you're not from the right family, even if you're white, forget it. But to entertain clients, there's an advantage.

"There are limits in social contact. A lot of things I talk only to blacks about. You just can't open up to whites as much. You have to pick and choose. But blacks can talk to other blacks, or complain about little things and feel comfortable, and not be tagged."

Art Barlow

"Be with your staff and your boss. Lunch and barbecues build strong friendships. To lead, you need devotion. People won't want to let you down. In informal settings, problems get solved. So relate. Invite people to your house, and don't worry about going to theirs. Once they get to know you, you'll be fine. Too many blacks isolate themselves. So invite younger blacks into your networks. Don't let them be isolated."

Mode 2

Walt Thomas

"There was a going-away party. We gravitated to one area. But that makes them nervous. Some of the white folks drifted over to listen in on conversations, and eyed us curiously. Some socializing I'm excluded from. But I don't care. I know I'm missing something. But I'm not committed to this organization. I don't feel like paying the price, or I'd challenge it more."

Mel Wilson

"Some senior whites have club connections. But most don't get that perk until they arrive. So blacks aren't competing against people who really have that advantage. That complaint is just one more way to say life's unfair.

"Blacks don't get anywhere by kissing ass. But I'm joining a country club, and a city club, and some civic organizations. I'll be active and take a leadership role. I'll see if it helps generate insurance business. It's an experiment. My wife is not enthusiastic. But I tell her, 'If you keep saying no, they'll stop inviting you.' So we bring some social isolation on ourselves.

"Your marriage matters. It makes people see you positively. If you're single, they think you're 'out there' and not settled. They think, if you can manage a family, it's further evidence you can manage. Not being married earlier might have delayed my progress.

"Ingratiate yourself. Don't isolate yourself or be a wallflower. We'll go on the road. At the end of the day, a bunch go to the hotel bar. Too often, blacks opt out. 'Oh, I'll just stay in my room and read.' Hey, you can't do that. Mingle, informally get to know people. Let them know you. Of course, after a few drinks, some people's racism shows. And you might even have to get funky with them if it's offensive enough.

"It can be a catch-22. Speaking up about an incident can be a bad career move. But keeping quiet or, worse, laughing along with them, they don't respect that either. So I stay awhile, then exit gracefully, as early as I can. That's how you handle a lot of social requirements."

Ossie Gordon

"We were invited to parties. But we didn't reciprocate much. Our office was hierarchical and military. We entertained some but were never excluded. It made no difference in my advancement. It might have helped my working relationships. But to get to managing partner, you had to get caught up in the social aspect.

"I had more outside interests than the people I worked with, so I distanced. My partners were smart but narrow, one-dimensional. They knew computers, audits, whatever. I'm not a snob, but I'm interested in more in life. Golf and country clubs were not part of our culture."

Chris Simms, 44, is a manager in insurance.

"A good sense of humor helps in social situations. But many blacks who keep to themselves are better off. Don't reveal your lifestyle. But my attitude is in your face. Why hide the fact that we're buying a house in Potomac? Some will resent it, but tough. Of course, don't put your business in the street. But let some colleagues get to know you. Anyhow, you're damned if you do, damned if you don't. If you don't associate, you've 'got a bad attitude.'"

Adele Belmont

"I socialize with people I like. Otherwise, I don't. My boss, once a year, invited us to his big house in Connecticut. But I didn't like him, so I only went one year.

"You know that *Wall Street Journal* article about the black manager complaining he wasn't invited? That was stupid. If it was important, *he* should have invited *them*. Don't wait to initiate relationships. Invite people who outrank you. You'll see them, and be seen, in a different light.

"In investment banking, blacks hosted for tennis or golf. It's possible in any industry. At my boss's Christmas party one year, I met a guy and later called him for advice. But I wouldn't date at work because of downside risks if things go badly. You see them everyday."

Linda Jackson

"I'm closed out. I went to a party. A vice president invited me. I thought it was just dinner. The butler answered the door. It was a 'dinner at eight' scene. This is incongruent with my background. And my lifestyle is low-key. When blacks hit the ceiling, the social gap widens as your former peers are still climbing. Earlier, it was easier to socialize. If I were white, I'd be at the same career level, and the same social level as the folks I started with.

"Black people are adaptable. But whites aren't. They don't want to adjust to our culture or lifestyle. I went to another party last week. It wasn't just folks from our company. It was half black and half white. The blacks didn't know each other, but they related. But the whites went to one end and the blacks to the other."

Ward Hampton

"We don't have access to the same number of social contacts or events that expand your network as our colleagues. That makes life more difficult. Positive thoughts come out of familiarity. So, to move up, live where others in the firm live. I live in an IBM neighborhood. They cluster. So get in the right zip code. Many judgments are based on brief contacts in a particular setting. So be involved in community organizations—choral arts, theater, United Fund—so those contacts pull you into the right circles."

Bob York

"I can rise to top management. Mediocre white managers make it. But you don't have the social things going for you. You can't just make it on ability. Success requires more. Socializing with white managers, especially with technical backgrounds, isn't pleasant. But do some to move up."

Earl Newsome

"Socializing is a skill, a talent. I have it. But lots of managers, black and white, just can't hang. Be available and friendly but disinterested. If you lust after acceptance, people will find ways to frustrate you. On the other hand, maintain distance but without hostility. Self-possession can come across as antagonism.

"In my early thirties, I got involved with a lady at work who a lot of guys had their eyes on. But it led to antagonism. So be friendly, but don't be seen as having an unzipped fly. I like a good time. When the music starts, I like to dance. But social work relationships, even if platonic, arouse white men's sexual fantasies, and that invites problems."

Ted Weaver

"It's legitimate to look at social and sexual behavior. There can be racism in those evaluations. But a manager running amok, or indiscreet, or lustful, no matter how sharp, shows poor judgment. And it's not unfair or racist to hold it against him."

Mode 3

Steve Johnson, 35, is in computer sales in California.

"People can be treacherous after a few drinks and make ugly remarks. Incidents happen. Do the benefits justify the aggravation of socializing with people you'd rather have nothing to do with off the job?"

Walt Adkins, 53, manages an engineering laboratory.

"People share secrets. And so by socializing, you hear things. I'm not excluded. But I'm in a better position to manage by not socializing with subordinates. Some managers get in sticky situations with complex social relationships with staff. And I don't want my achievement tainted (with people feeling I had social advantages). I want to make it strictly on objective criteria."

Simon Trainor, 45, is an engineer in a large aerospace firm.

"I have no social contact off the job. We're at a disadvantage. No golf. No drinks. It can cost you a lot. But you can't force people to socialize."

Ben Collins, 43, is a VP in a large Philadelphia bank.

"People get hung up on it. They think it's the most important thing. I disagree. It's nice, but most don't get much out of partying with associates. Do the job. I don't feel pressure to socialize.

"Sales might require it, but not many other functions. And if you get a position because of social contacts, you're dependent on that goodwill. And that's a tenuous spot. It's natural for us to be at a disadvantage after five o'clock. The brother says to himself, 'I don't want to get close because they just want to get into my business.' And the others aren't really comfortable with us. So both tend to distance."

Joe Wilson

"I decided early that if social activity was important to get ahead, I didn't want it. I don't socialize with people I work with. Certain functions you have to make. And I fraternize at lunch. But I've avoided companies where that's expected.

"Too many black managers make it seem crucial. I want to get ahead strictly on performance. If you go up on social connections, you can go down on them. Don't get me wrong. People have to feel you belong. When I was younger, I enjoyed playing softball and basketball, and a drink after work. But that was the reason. I enjoyed it. Now, I don't want to be in the country club."

11

Gaining Maturity,
Emotional Growth,
and Awareness

"The meeting of two personalities is like the contact of two chemical substances: if there is any reaction, both are transformed."

CARL JUNG

"Mental health problems do not affect three out of every five persons, but one out of one."

KARL MENNINGER

"I always live by this simple rule, whatever happens, don't lose your cool."

OSCAR BROWN JR.

Organizations Provoke Anger

There are four basic emotions: love, fear, anger, and pain. Most we aren't allowed to express at work. But the one that surfaces most is anger. Managing all of them can require awareness and an investment in developing coping skills.

Anger begets anger, and criticism provokes criticism—especially in the workplace. These and other negative behaviors arise out of a desire to control others. And that's a formula for frustration and defeat. You can only control yourself—and that only if you work at it. So detach yourself from the losing struggle to change others, and change yourself.

If your interactions too frequently turn angry, associates will avoid you, exclude you, and withhold rewards. You, in turn, will feel alienated. There'll be a downward spiral. Finally, you'll leave or become ineffective. So become aware of what drives you. Continue to educate yourself about organizational behavior, through courses, books, and therapy or counseling.

With clear personal goals and a realistic strategy, you'll feel better about your situation. You'll work with associates and staff more harmoniously because you'll feel in charge of your destiny. You can only control yourself and your own decisions—when you try and fail to control others' behavior, you will feel defeated. Then conflicts will happen more readily and you can find yourself in a chronically angry or antagonistic mode.

What You Can Do

When organizations or managers become too negatively emotional or oppressive, they are sources of injustice. Then members withdraw, go low-profile, and hunker down to protect themselves. That diminishes effectiveness. But many firms and executives unwittingly produce such counterproductive behavior.

Many managers—black *and* white—violate their own basic values to get ahead. They sell their souls. So review what you believe. Don't let pressures make you act contrary to what you are, creating negative feelings.

Some managers seek success, power, and status by mistreating others. They generate emotional responses. But managers who understand themselves can lead with more emotional integrity and get along with all sorts of colleagues. So it becomes important to invest in self-awareness. That's the best way to insure that the emotional dimension of life won't cause undue problems.

Managing Anxiety and Anger

An *Industry Week* survey finds middle managers feeling anxious and afraid. They believe corporate moves to become lean have been excessively mean, so it will be hard to maintain or restore commitments to organization welfare as long as top management seems callous and brutal. The Hay Group surveys professionals, managers, clericals, and hourly staffers on job satisfaction. A continuing reality is that managers and professionals in Vanguard companies report higher satisfaction than managers in industries like steel and automotives, perceived as Old Guard and not as innovative in organizing and treating people. In intellectually stimulating environments, where intrinsic satisfaction is higher, you can accept and live with irritations. Racial conflicts that produce rage in an Old Guard bureaucracy can be tolerated in a Vanguard environment.

Frustrations sometimes have racial overtones, but there's seldom anything clear-cut. Slights, indignities, offenses get to you. But you can't explode. And even communicating anger by facial expression, body language, or distancing can threaten. Venting is not good, but neither is repressing feelings.

Avoid becoming angry so often in the first place. Roll with the punches more. How you think about comments and incidents largely determines what you feel about them.

Opinion Research says most senior managers are "afraid to share feelings about problems." Managers, generally, are afraid to be candid. But African-American managers often complain about and criticize their companies on racial grounds. This tendency to express negative feelings about perceived injustices gets them labeled as troublemakers, boat rockers, and malcontents.

Fast-growth firms, according to Hay, treat people with more respect than slow-growth firms. And they offer more satisfaction, rewards, and justice. In such firms, 60 percent of employees, including managers, felt respected. But, in slow-growth firms, although 60 percent of managers felt respected, only 30 percent of professional and 40 percent of clericals felt respected. Ninety percent of all respondents felt satisfied with their jobs, and 80 percent with their companies. So many managers find intrinsic satisfaction that overcomes irritations.

Thomas Kochman, in his book, *Black and White Styles in Conflict*, says that office communication interracially breaks down because blacks often value confrontation and argument. And they become emotional as a way to "seek the truth." He believes that to black managers, confronting someone shows caring enough to want to settle a dispute rather than let it ride. Whites, on the other hand, avoid confrontation. They believe it is bad form, shows disunity, and could lead to an actual physical fight. But most African Americans who feel anger handle it assertively in a straightforward, factual, nonthreatening way.

Rage, that nearly out-of-control feeling, can lead to problems. And organizational injustices do push some managers to rage. That's why the more you learn about yourself and your motivations and reactions, the better. You can feel rage when you don't meet your own expectations and performance standards. But a balanced life involving outside activities like sports, music, and other diversions will help you manage those situations at work.

Managers who are angry often look to settle scores. That's a major activity in many Old Guard companies. They harbor resentments and look for payback. But revenge becomes a cycle, because what goes around comes around. Trying to get even is self-destructive. You can get short-term satisfaction, but what if you have to depend on your victims, or their friends, later?

Manage Your Feelings and Stress

To work effectively, promote harmony, and reduce hostility, rivalries, resentment, miscommunication, abrasion, and mistrust, you must manage your feelings. Here are ways to stay in step:

- Tell the truth.
- Communicate carefully what you're feeling using "I" messages.
- Keep commitments.

- Back up teammates to get the job done, even if you have reservations about the direction.
- Tell others how they come across to you—without blaming them.
- Don't make *them* wrong and *yourself* right.
- Don't bad-mouth the company.
- Complain only in private, and only to someone who can do something about it, not to relieve frustration to just anyone who will listen.

Psychologist Bruce Baldwin offers a way to manage stresses you'll experience compounded by racial injustices. His book *It's All in Your Head: Lifestyle Management Strategies for Busy People* outlines three principles:

1. Stress distorts reality and makes it harder to cope intelligently.
2. Stress makes you more compulsive and mistake prone.
3. As stress rises, self-esteem falls, because under stress you're likely to say and do things you wouldn't otherwise say or do.

When you're under stress:

- Memory and concentration fail.
- You exaggerate problems.
- Your attention span is shorter.
- Your mind races, and your thoughts are jumbled.
- You dwell on negative ideas.
- You become stubborn and inflexible.
- You become hypercritical.
- You feel like a victim.
- You lose your sense of humor.
- You become more demanding.
- You don't plan well.
- You try to escape reality and fantasize more.

Baldwin advises:

1. Don't react spontaneously. Physically, emotionally, and intellectually distance to put matters in perspective.

2. Accept what you can't do anything about. And be realistic about what you can change.

3. Get the facts. Don't assume bad motives.

4. Think of alternative responses.

5. Think positively. Your feelings are influenced by how you think about events.

Get to Know Yourself

Develop positive habits to deal with stress and conflicts. That's why it is necessary to invest in professional counseling and therapy. To cope with stress and other negative events and feelings, you need to be able to think constructively about troubling incidents, not as a victim. To manage emotions well, self-awareness is key. And that requires disclosure best practiced in the safety of good therapy, because most of us can't expose feelings well. We hide them, or we blurt them out at inopportune times. So to learn how to reveal what you feel, confide in a professional you trust who can educate you on emotional management.

Most people have some neurosis, a problem of the mind or emotions that involves anxiety, phobias, or fears, or other dysfunctional behavior with no physical basis. These are mild conditions, but they can be self-defeating, so you need to get to understand the ways you think and behave that are not in your rational best interests. Counseling helps you eliminate habits of mind and reaction patterns that keep you from reaching objectives. It helps you see that you play a role in creating difficulties for yourself. Too many people learn bad habits early in life for dealing with adversaries and competitors. Therapy gives them insights, understanding, and the ability to change.

Use Myers-Briggs

The Myers-Briggs Type Indicator (MBTI) is a paper-and-pencil test that takes thirty minutes. It helps you understand your natural biases in approaching life's situations. You rely primarily on intuition, thinking, feeling, or sensing in dealing with issues, people, and problems. Knowing your tendencies puts you in a better position to figure out how to get on with people of other types, so goes the theory.

Many counselors and human resource specialists apparently find the MBTI valid, and it helps managers function with clearer knowledge of their makeup. You need every tool available for managing the emotional side of the job. Knowing how your personal style differs from your associates' can help you avoid assuming racial motives when there's conflict over specific issues. Many, and perhaps most, emotional conflicts result from people just being the way they are—nothing racist about it. Knowing that can help you avoid mistakes, prejudgments, false conclusions about motivation, and damaging incidents.

Marjorie White and Marcella Wiener, who wrote *The Theory and Practice of Self-Psychology*, find that many people in all occupations are deprived of admiration, applause, and good models. Confidence and self-esteem are based on positive feedback all through life, but many managers never get this. Managers need appreciation, cheers, and fans. Lack of appreciation is a continuing burden.

Many managers are chronically angry because when they were young, an adult they depended on, especially a parent, turn out to be unreliable. That leads to cynicism and a hypercritical attitude. If we can examine these kinds of experiences with professional help, we can overcome such problems and their impact on our performance.

We can also be a victim of corporate or self-imposed pressure to succeed. That can lead to depression. Again, self-examination can be the remedy. A 1984 study at Penn State found "excellent" managers are competitive, aggressive, impatient, have trouble delegating, and have few outside interests. They're unbalanced and lopsided. But this isn't a useful definition of *excellent* except in the stereotyped sense of "driven." That's not what *excellent* should mean. *Excellent* should include being emotionally healthy, nurturing, supporting, and inspiring. And that level of all around good functioning often requires an investment in counseling.

You have unconscious motivations and you need approval, recognition, affiliation, trust, and probably also competition. You may also have rivalry and dependency needs. Understand what makes you tick, and you'll manage more effectively. Paula Bernstein's *Family Ties, Corporate Bonds* says if you act out your early family experience in business life, it can be either destructive *or* positive. Many actions, good and bad, are based unconsciously on unresolved childhood experiences.

Middle managers are part of a large age cohort used to heavy competition at home, at school, and in careers. Many engage in a kind of sibling rivalry in dealing with colleagues. You'll trigger unconscious resentments in some people, apart from race, because of these unresolved parent or sibling issues. And you, too, may respond to cues unconsciously. So training, reading, reflection, and counseling will help prepare you so you won't be blindsided by such unconscious factors.

Douglas LaBier, with the Project on Technology, Work and Character, and Otto Kernberg, of the Cornell Medical Center, outline several types of managers:

Schizoid
- emotionally isolated
- not tuned to associates' feelings
- perceived by subordinates as distant and aloof
- leaves others feeling isolated
- offers staff independence and autonomy

Obsessive
- follows rules mechanically and stifles creativity
- inflexible when a crisis needs imagination
- can be sadistic and vengeful, forcing creative staffers to leave and retaining those who seek security
- excellent attention to detail
- precise and clear decisions
- efficient

Narcissistic
- excessively self-centered

No doubt in your training you've had an exercise in which you typed yourself. There are many such management typologies. Here, for example, is one: LIFO, or Life Orientation Outline. Many companies use it.

Supporting/Giving	You work hard and pursue excellence, and you believe this will bring you rewards.
Conserving/Holding	You think before you act, and you make the most of what you have.
Controlling/Taking	You seek results by seizing opportunities and through competence.
Adapting/Dealing	You seek to please others and to meet their needs.

The trouble is most managers do the drill and perhaps find a label that applies, but never really learn much about their own specific motivations and patterns that may be useful in helping them change. That can really only come from a long-term commitment and continuing attention to personal growth.

You have some special pressures because of race. So you have an extra incentive to make the commitment to take care of yourself. Pay attention to psychological information and you'll remain emotionally healthy and effective. It's when you let yourself get compulsive and obsessed, out of balance, or as some call it, codependent, that performance can slip. At times like that, relationships with staff, bosses, and coworkers can deteriorate. Then you can fail to see clues and fall into a destructive conflict.

Handle Mid-Life Gracefully

Much complaining by black managers about ceilings and plateaus comes from people thirty-five to fifty-five. This is an age when managers who haven't realized their goals are feeling bad about the fact that they must come to terms with the reality that they aren't going to become partner or director or vice president as they had once hoped. It's also a time when you're not the bright young fast-track candidate anymore, if you ever were. And compliments and encouragement have stopped coming.

These feelings may be compounded by race. But mid-life can be generally rough on emotions. Getting reassurance can be difficult, too. By mid-career, it's natural to think you can handle more responsibility and get recognition, visibility, and authority. But if that doesn't happen, you can become bitter.

So understand that in mid-career you may get fewer strokes. Knowing this should help you avoid getting angry, demoralized, depressed, and feeling like a victim of simple racial discrimination. Between thirty-five and fifty-five we tend to experience some such internal discomfort because we're dissatisfied with what we have accomplished. But usually the bad mood passes, and we get on with our lives with a revised perspective and agenda.

You have home and family concerns. You're not the athlete you used to be. Your parents may get sick and die. Your children are teenagers with problems. If you run into a mid-life rough period, you don't just have to accept it. You may need help getting through all this. You may get busier at work in charities or church and community activities. But some get into alcohol or other addictive behavior. Counseling is rewarding in tough situations, above and beyond its value for management development. So are a wide variety of twelve-step programs that offer continuing opportunities for reflection, feedback, and growth.

So to handle mid-career and mid-life issues, concentrate on the task, on mastery and expertise. Add value. Get satisfactions outside. Work on the problems that you present to others rather than focusing on the problems they present to you. Recognize that hitting a ceiling or plateau is the norm. You aren't a special victim.

You can reevaluate your whole approach to career and rebalance life and work. You can choose family, the arts, community, or social services when you decide to shift your primary commitment from career focus to a broader one. The key is, be aware that you can *choose*.

Go for training in self-awareness and in teambuilding and interpersonal relations. You were exposed to these concepts in school. But these skills are important enough to make them a matter of lifelong learning. When people say blacks need to be "better" than whites to get equal rewards, they usually don't have this dimension in mind. But in this realm, extra effort pays dividends.

The Modes and How They Manage Emotions

Mode 1 managers believe blacks have to keep it buttoned up and buttoned down at all costs. They have learned to work with Old Boys and Yammies by setting aside value discrepancies. They generally feel at ease with associates and adapt and maintain an even temper. They believe professionalism and racial realities both require getting along despite subtle offenses. They deny that provocations are racial—or they acknowledge the possibility but insist they aren't bothered or are above being annoyed. Denial is a key defense mechanism. They verbalize anger when directly attacked or victimized but hold their peace if others are the target. They seldom directly intervene if they see a racial injustice.

Mode 2 managers acknowledge much more anger at injustice but also avoid reacting. They don't deny the feelings provoked. They concentrate on production and make allowances for colleagues by pointing out the realities and complexities of interracial teamwork. They deal with their anger by mature rational distancing and careful selection of informal associates. They are formal in most dealings and avoid situations that could deteriorate. They also avoid involvement on behalf of others when there's an injustice.

Mode 3 managers are more frequently angry. They can handle offenses diplomatically, but they're more frequently offended and see hostile acts more readily. They're more likely to confront and verbalize displeasure when there are offenses and injustices to themselves and when they see others having problems. Thus, they are most likely to be seen as having "a chip on their shoulder."

Mode 1

Adele Belmont

"I survive bad situations by putting on a facade. I don't let people see my feelings. When I'm mad, I distance and get quiet. I don't express anger, because I'm not good at it. Oh, I might fly off the handle and say something in irritation, and I might say I don't like what's happening. But basically I back off. I'm not sure those are mature, professional responses, but they're healthy. I let off steam by talking to my boss, who's also black.

"Once I had to work with someone I thoroughly disliked. He didn't like having a younger black female in the job. We were equals, so I let my attitude show. But as a subordinate, I keep my mouth shut and go about my business."

Stu Elmore

"If I get mad, I decide how to react. Everybody displays something, sometime. And some colleagues try to get a rise. They get under your skin and say to themselves 'Hey. That's fun. Let's do it again.' But you can't think clearly when angry. Don't show it. I never react. I count to 145. Cool out. Take a walk. Avoid confrontations. Don't jump in someone's face. And don't try to get even. Most troublemakers crucify themselves if you leave them alone."

Mode 2

Joe Wilson

"I have a good wife or I wouldn't have made it to senior management. She reassures me. You see people moving faster, passing you by. And you need someone to talk to. I pour out my frustrations. She dries the tears and tells me I'm great. She's like a second, a cornerman in boxing. But if homelife is tough, you won't be ready for the next round at work. If you also have to duke it out at home, you're in trouble. So it's important to have a solid home life."

Art Clark, 35, is an auditor in a large accounting firm.

"I do get upset, but my apparent peace of mind comes from being a Christian. A sense of purpose helps. Diversify your psychological investments so your ego isn't totally on the line in your job.

"When something happens, I'm no less pissed. But I leave it and go home, kiss my baby, my wife, and get satisfaction outside of work. What bothers me most is when it's my fault. But I say, 'Hey. I screwed up. I'll do better next time.' If it's something I can't do anything about, I keep on trucking.

"I assume people have good intentions. Results may not be good because they have poor information or bad priorities or unconscious drives—that's how I look at racism. Maybe that's naive. Some people, without realizing it, use phrases that push buttons, trigger reactions. Language habits cause lots of problems."

Brad Graham

"People don't deal with problems. They sweep them under the rug. It's, 'Let's not be emotional. Let's not hold grudges.' So no one admits there's racism. When I'm angry, it has to come out. So I talk to myself. I pace the floor if it's a situation where showing anger would show weakness. I talk to my wife or friends I trust. But it's not good to show anger. It's irrational and unprofessional. If things can upset you, it means you aren't mature and can't be trusted. But if someone confronts you in public, respond. But if you lose your temper, you hurt your image and lose points."

Mel Wilson

"The level of civility is high. The code is, don't show feelings. You win some. You lose some. You don't invest so much emotion in one transaction that if it goes against you you lose it. There are always more transactions. American management style is cool. Emotionless is what it means to be professional.

But people have different views and interpretations of facts and situations. And that leads to conflict, black and black, black and white, white and white. But some people assume blacks will automatically harmonize with other blacks. Wrong. Conflicts and rivalry is normal because resources are scarce. Others want what you want."

Earl Newsome

"Be authentic and objective. See things for what they are, and if you're angry, look them in the eye and nonverbally convey your feelings. Use body language and facial expressions, then, if necessary, get verbal. But usually, only talk about it if a problem becomes extreme.

"I'm living in *their* family, not my own. So learn to live with negative feelings. That's the way it is. Part of the program in cross-cultural relationships is strain. It's not a loving relationship. It's not a weekend with your paramour. Play the hand you're dealt. Understand yourself. Don't ask for lollipops when they're handing out snowballs. As Kennedy said, 'Fair is a child's word.' I will not dip my flag. But I can talk to people I can't stand. It's important to be able to do that, but too many black managers can't bring themselves to do it."

Thelma Morris

"Two engineers were arguing. One wouldn't approve something. The other guy says. 'Hey. Yesterday your boss said he'd clear it.' So both go higher to get it resolved reasonably with compromise, negotiation. I can usually settle issues. But in these situations—an impasse—I talk to them separately.

"Only if you know you'll have no future dealings can you let negative feelings show. But when I got an unjust evaluation, I said what I felt, and my boss just said, 'That's how it goes.'

"My emotions are triggered when some client gets on my case and they're wrong. I get steamed. I let a guy have it yesterday. He put me on the defensive. Then he offered to take me to lunch. I said, 'Here's constructive criticism. Don't be so critical.' If I hadn't composed myself, I would have hung up on him. I said, 'You were ranting and raving. And your tone was nasty. In the future, don't do that.' "

Art Barlow

"I don't go off when I get angry. I stutter. Besides, if you're angry, someone else probably is, too. So I get quiet, and everyone else calms down, too. One client went off in a meeting. Threw a paper clip at me. I left the room. Twenty minutes later, he apologized. And our firm got more business. But he was a liberal, and felt bad."

Jim Waters

"At our major client, I threaten their notions about black folk. The key guy said, 'I like you as a human being,' implying he had problems with me professionally. But that doesn't bother me. I could have gotten mad, frustrated, and belligerent. But I stay focused on quality. I hear comments, process them, and focus on the task.

"My wife and friends understand my predicament. I talk candidly with white and black members of my staff. And I keep a Bible in my office. Some people start the day without God. But He's an integral part of my life. So I pray before I leave home and read the Bible on the train to work. Many people are tired and strained starting the day. I start fresh. But misery loves company. Lots of people try to drag you down. I don't like to be around people like that. Faith, trust, and belief overwhelm negativism, anxiety, worry, and fear. Don't leave home without Him. That's how I deal with it."

Louise Gibson

"When people go off, I get calm. It works. Some are totally into gut emotion. But I'm quiet, thoughtful. I may get pissed off, but I'm cool. If it's a political issue, I vent only to my manager. In a way that shows concern about the team, not just myself. That's constructive.

"Creative people use emotional rhetoric. But I don't like it. When folks let emotions get the best of them, competing with me, I usually come out on top."

Polly Simmons, 46, is a lawyer with a major firm. She's been a manager in federal and municipal agencies.

"I internalize a lot. I don't let you know I'm upset. I'm hard-nosed and thick-skinned but sensitive to subordinates' feelings. I'm no more touchy than whites. But certain signals based on history and culture get to me.

"When I'm angry, I stay rational. I'm not self-destructive, so I won't explode. But I'm vocal when something is handled poorly. I'm lucky—I command respect, and people respond. So, if I'm emotional, people respond. I never have to act out. I have status based on performance, so people listen to my concerns. Outbursts occur when people feel frustrated because their views aren't respected. And that sets up incidents that break down relations. I enjoy work. It's never boring. If you have that, you won't be bent out of shape by problems."

Bud Martin, 37, is a hospital administrator.

"I cry on the inside sometimes. But I don't show it. I'm not intimidating. I'm passive, and I'm not inclined to do anything when offended. My wife, a lawyer, says I have a fragile ego. I'm more sensitive than I should be. But if you're not ready for hassles, you're not really ready to play the game."

Alan Roland

"A sense of humor is a key to success. If you react to every incident, you're branded as aggressive or argumentative. Lots of black managers have a chip on their shoulders because of earlier experiences. But you can go too far the other way, too, accommodating and understanding. Then you're seen as an Uncle

Tom—and that's worse. When you react to offenses, they fear you. But Toms get no respect."

Cecil Clemens

"We tend to be more emotional and open. I care a lot about unjust situations and people. But there's not as high a concern among my colleagues. I'm circumspect, deliberate, calm, and cool. I have a more excitable personality than I show. Blacks, like Italians, are more demonstrative. And we have to cool it.

"We were analyzing financial and management systems in a $30 billion portfolio for this client. I had ten staffers on site. A manager at the client asked me into his office, without any of my staff. I started to take notes, and he said, 'It's off the record.' So I put down my pen. He said, 'Are you guys paid by the things you find wrong, the more money you get?' I was taken aback. I operate under rules of the AICPA (American Institute of CPAs) and other guidelines. There are checks and cross-checks.

"The guy was impugning my motives and the results. It was personal and also attacked the firm. I thought it was unprofessional. I was furious. He could challenge a technical point. No problem. You present evidence, and I present mine. That's fine. But he's coming after me. I'm ready to fight, almost like he'd said something about my mama. But I calmed down and said to myself, 'I'll be very careful how I deal with this man.' On the street, provocations like that lead to trouble. So we learn to be deliberate.

"These incidents occur too often. Willie Horton is every white's fantasy of the black bad guy. And whites worry about black male assault. So they feel threatened by me, a Stanford grad, in a way. And white females are also wary and less communicative. In my downtown office, there's a woman CPA—warm, friendly. Next door, another woman CPA ignores me. I say, 'Hi,' and get back nothing. Both are married, as am I. Cultural background explains why one is friendly and the other not.

"We have more work than we can handle. Everybody's busy. There's no b.s. The culture is, get to the point. But I talk a lot and schmooze. So I had to learn to be brief with personal stuff. Blacks tend to be verbal. We tend to have academic majors in social sciences, where talk is rewarded. But in business, time is money. Don't tie up a colleague's time. Sometimes they kick back and want to rap. It's their option. That's okay. But we also tend to think we're right on issues. My wife jokes, 'We be ego-centric.' So sort out the factors causing trouble. Get a third-party opinion.

"Familiarity can also breed contempt. When blacks are too friendly sometimes, we're seen as weak. People try to take advantage. So I take account of whether incidents happen because I'm black or because I am too friendly, too familiar, maybe."

Mode 3

Paul Allen, 40, is a manager in a large transportation firm.

"Black managers are more emotional. They gripe overtly and are more caustic in confrontations."

Harry Nelson

"I have a contribution to make. But the corporation is giving me a raw deal. It pisses me off the way I'm stymied. And I tell people how I feel. I got hurt in Vietnam in an explosion. And I have high blood pressure. This situation with these racist games contributes to these health problems. But I keep my sense of humor and perspective and don't get hostile."

Wes Albright

"My boss complained that we'd argued in front of other people, that I'd yelled at him and slammed the phone on another occasion. Both true. But I told him he shouldn't fear expressions of anger. It's natural. I say what I feel. Then I get over it. But most people suppress it. And then it gets into games. One incident doesn't make them bad people. We can still have a relationship.

"I pay a price for being spontaneous. So I do less of it than I used to. I see fewer things as affronts. And when I'm angry, I often don't say what needs to be said. I keep composure to focus on issues. But willful prevarication triggers anger. They know and I know they're lying. And I don't get angry at failure. But I do at laziness."

Bill Tompkins

"I've gone off, but less and less. My boss even said, 'I can swallow an elephant, but I bite at flies.' They see me handle big problems but go off on little things. Swallow hard and ignore things. But I retaliate by not cooperating and not explaining why this or that didn't work.

"I ventilate with peers who understand the big picture, the delicate nature of race relations here, and know the players, so they can tell if my reaction to some incident is right or off the wall. But people who give honest feedback are hard to find."

Walt Thomas

"I get self-righteous and angry too easily. One guy gave me grief on the phone, then hung up. I called back and said, 'Don't do that again.' And he hasn't. He was testing me. When people go off on you, it's usually not personal. It's what you're saying in your role they react to. So depersonalize it in your own mind.

"We have a surgeon here. Notoriously rude, abusive, and childish. I asked her about some space changes. She started to curse, shout, then cry. I left. If she does that again, I'll say, 'When you get control of yourself, I'll come back, and we'll talk.'"

12

Staying in Sync With Other Black Managers

"I am the greatest."

MUHAMMAD ALI

"Where all think alike, no one thinks very much."

WALTER LIPPMANN

"We must try to trust one another. Stay and cooperate."

JOMO KENYATTA

"Try a little tenderness."

OTIS REDDING

There's a general assumption that black managers trust, cooperate with, and support each other. But too often that's wishful thinking. Disappointments are frequent, and trust, too often, is misplaced.

One reason is that black managers, like all managers, have different modes of thinking and operating. So there's no reason to assume automatic, inherent fellow-feeling. It's unrealistic to expect strong differences in philosophy, personality, and perceived self-interest to be overcome based on romantic notions of nationalistic or racial solidarity.

196

The bottom line is that you should approach other African Americans case by case. Evaluate and judge individuals on their merits, and look for ways to support them.

Cooperate, Support, Respect, and Admire

These actions are crucial. You won't fully achieve, lead, and enjoy all the rewards of management until African-American managers, in general, have confidence and credibility and are seen as a competitive asset. But for black managers to see themselves and be seen that way, they first need confidence in each other and must enjoy each other's full professional respect. That won't happen through exhortation. That will only happen as confidence is earned, as talent and results are demonstrated.

We hear complaints about black movie stars and athletes choosing white agents and lawyers. There are complex reasons, including status. But there is also risk aversion—a fear of disappointment. They assume that established whites are more likely to produce the desired results than relatively less experienced blacks. "Their ice is colder," as the saying goes.

African Americans have to overcome internal credibility gaps before general credibility can be completely established. So earn other black managers' confidence. In a sense, that's the top priority. Earning their admiration will be a real achievement, and the benefits will spill over.

What You Can Do

Don't Assume Automatic Solidarity

Black managers can often find greater support and coaching from Solids than from other black managers. And they can have more confidence in some Solids than in other black managers. But cohesion is building, and mutual confidence is growing.

There's often a kind of tipping point that produces odd behavior in blacks and whites. Some black managers get uneasy when there are "too many" because they've gotten used to standing out. And that can produce dangerous game playing. But in time this phase will end. In many Vanguard companies, it already has. In more and more companies, black managers work successfully in the same unit. But you can't assume it. The degree of trustworthiness has to be established by trial and error as in any other relationship.

Beware of Crabs in the Barrel

The image of crabs in the barrel is one way of envisioning collusion. In this psychological picture, members of a unit conspire unconsciously *not* to excel, *not* to outdo each other, *not* to stand out or draw attention to themselves. It makes them secure, in a way. But it keeps performance mediocre. Group members seem equal. But the able members are kept from achieving much.

In some settings, black managers do this, too. Guard against it. Acting out crabs in the barrel makes life even more treacherous. Clarence McKee, a director of the Reagan-Bush campaign in 1984 in the District of Columbia, says, "It's unfortunate that many black Republicans spend their time doing end runs around other blacks. They are ineffective because they spend so much time in petty jealousies and rivalries."

Look for Opportunities to Encourage

To improve your progress and strengthen other black mangers, applaud, approve, cheer, congratulate. Most managers do this too infrequently. Show confidence. Find someone's good performance on a proposal, project, analysis, insight, presentation, decision, whatever. Be a positive reinforcer.

Make the Most of the NBA Effect

African-American managers are gravitating in disproportionate numbers to certain industries and certain functions. For example, banking, office equipment, some consumer goods, and financial services are favored. And finance, marketing, human resources, employee, community, government, and public relations are the areas where they work. There's still underrepresentation in engineering, high technology, operations/production, natural resources, and basic manufacturing line management.

This tendency to agglomerate is the NBA Effect. Remember how Wilt Chamberlain, Bill Russell, Oscar Robertson, Connie Hawkins, Elgin Baylor, Earl Monroe, and Julius Erving innovated and changed basketball? Something like that may happen. There are indications that black managers will change the way business is done and the way organizations are managed, in industries and functions where there is room for a kind of cultural impact.

In time, even Old Boys and Yammies will imitate some of the innovations, which will then become part of normal management practice. Business will be enriched. To use a biological analogy, there'll be a kind of hybrid vigor.

Treat Each Other With Respect and Common Courtesy

One important dimension of group respect is basic courtesy. And perhaps the most noted area of breakdown is in telephone communication. Answer your own phone, and return all calls promptly. Too many black managers get careless and discourteous about these matters. Time is money. Don't waste yours or other people's. Don't have your secretary place calls, then let other people wait for you to come on the line. It may subtly establish status rankings, but it damages mutual respect.

For incoming calls, don't let callers wait while you finish what you're doing. Respect their time. If you're really in the middle of something important, then, of course, let someone else handle it. But most meetings and conversations aren't really crucial. You can interrupt them. Games are played around who calls whom, who waits for whom, who calls whom first. All these undermine relations between black managers.

Suppose there's a problem, and you don't want to return a call because you don't want to deal with the issue. Then call and say so. Don't avoid the issue by not returning the call. We need less pettiness among us.

Network

The National Black MBA Association (NBMBAA) deserves wide support. (It should probably change its name to the National Management Association—the NBMBAA is awkward.) Its value depends on managers' willingness to reciprocate by sharing information, contacts, and introductions. But the best-placed, ablest, and most likely to succeed—the High Drafts and Blue Chips— steer clear and don't participate. That's an old, too common, story.

Explanations vary. But some conclude that individual talent and personal qualities alone got them where they are. This distancing reduces collective leverage. In any minority group, those who make it tend to be hyperindividualists.

On the other hand, the most able and astute resent others who behave like parasites. Some people use networking as a substitute for preparation, commitment, and hard work. They misuse personal contacts and favors such as introductions. The relatively less talented and successful may prey on the more successful to the point that the strongest avoid the network, making it less effective than it could be.

Maybe there's no solution. The best and brightest prefer to network with others like themselves. But leaders of professional, alumni, and other organizations need to find inducements to involve the most talented.

One key is high program quality. Don't let meetings deteriorate into low-level socializing and time wasting. Respecting each other is key to collective progress and to insuring the maximum soul in management.

There's been significant progress since the doors began to open in the mid 1960s. Thirty years of entry, development and demonstrated talent have landed more than a few black managers in senior line and staff jobs. The insecurities of pioneering can now be a thing of the past. The next thirty years will be more rewarding if we consciously develop appropriate mutual support and give full recognition to excellent achievement.

The Modes and How They View Black Managers

Mode 1 managers say individual black managers have been reliable and credible, but on occasion they've been disappointed or even hurt, accidentally or deliberately. And they hesitate to trust. They find personality differences often insurmountable. They think the competitiveness, rivalry, crabs-in-the-barrel impulses are still strong and create frequent barriers to cooperation. They're individualistic and say they believe it's a matter of the best rising strictly on merit.

Mode 2 managers say cooperation is key, and they go out of their way to try to establish good, mutually supportive relations. They've been burned a few times and are careful until trust is established. But they believe group effort matters and are willing to join groups and act collectively in a diplomatic and nonthreatening way to achieve common objectives.

Mode 3 managers believe little can be accomplished for most black managers without solidarity, networking, and support. They recognize that many don't share that view and even avoid close cooperation and identification. And they also know that rivalries drive wedges into potential black associations. But they're committed to working together, believing it's practical and essential.

Mode 1

Stu Elmore

"We don't share enough about experiences of organizational realities, power plays, that kind of stuff. So we tend to miss the big picture. We tend to be lone rangers because of the circumstances we've come through.

" 'Out of the jungle. Their own people sold them.' It will take time to trust. We've lost the ability to be together. There's still a battle for survival. All it will take is one deep depression, or twenty years of Reaganism, and we'd be set back. But a morsel of goodies, some affluence, has misled a lot of people into thinking they've made it personally.

"I've had as much trouble and negatives with blacks as with anyone else. And I've had whites warn me I shouldn't trust certain blacks. Loyalty is full-time, not just nine to five. It turns out they really were backstabbing. The whites were telling the truth.

"Some blacks who were untrustworthy I distanced from. Some I moved out of my organization. Handle it case by case. You can't generalize. People who don't work well with you usually have other problems and don't understand themselves. Often, they have troubled lives, and this is just one manifestation. Try to understand their problems."

Len Crandall

"Blacks avoid blacks because they think racial neutrality is expected. So they go out of their way to distance, to avoid seeming preferential. And some pretend you're just another person. Then there's no camaraderie."

Jane Allen, 37, is a manager in communications.

"I respect only a few blacks in this field completely, because too many try to get ahead on self-promotion. One guy is loud, aggressive, and avoids the grunt work. I look for substance. You can be a flash in this field of communications or a long-term player. But too many blacks seem lazy or shortsighted. So far, we've all made it to about the same level. But the day of reckoning hasn't come. There are show horses and work horses. I choose to be a work horse.

"Some rely on being black or politicking to get ahead. Instead, they should know what they're doing and do the job. But merit doesn't always win and produce fair rewards. I have to be able to sleep at night. I have a strong strict moral code that few share. Those who do I respect tremendously."

Mode 2

Gene Martin

"If you work for a brother, he'll give you more opportunity to try, fail, and learn. Whites have that opportunity, but we only have two chances to fail—and only one if they want to build a case. But some black managers put needlessly tough tests on black subordinates. It's the old story—I came up the hard way, and you should, too. It's the father who coaches Little League and tries to show he's not partial by being extra tough on his own son."

Adele Belmont

"Blacks don't adequately support other blacks. My boss didn't stand up for me to make sure I had a substantive involvement. He stabbed me in the back more than the previous white guy. It didn't matter to him, when it came time to reorganize, that I was black. It could have been handled differently, with less negative impact on me and others. Oh, he increased my salary, but not my role."

Bob York

"I had a black subordinate. And he had a black subordinate I wanted to terminate. He had been playing with his expense accounts, rental cars, and so on. I went to human resources, who told me I couldn't because of affirmative action, etc. Maybe he thought we'd let him slide because his boss and I were black. But I look at things as if I owned the business. I ask myself, does the behavior harm the business?

"The basic problem was, he was misslotted as a manager. He's technically sound. But he can't manage. So I talk to him. Actually, if it had been somebody else in my position, he'd probably have had his head chopped off earlier. But my boss is a fan of his. Sooner or later, though, something's going to jump up and bite him in the ass. He needs a good executive assistant to take care of things and keep him out of trouble."

Walt Thomas

"Whites are threatened that black mangers might unite. Eighty percent of our customers are black. If we united, they seem to feel we would gradually use our leverage to change things, and some of them might be out of a job.

"Whites give lip service to teamwork, but they're only loyal to themselves. So blacks shouldn't feel bashful about putting blacks into key jobs, assuming quality is there."

Thelma Morris, 45, works in a high-pressure public sector job that requires frequent contact and negotiations with corporate representatives on high-risk, high-reward projects.

"Working with and for black managers can be stimulating and exasperating. A new black manager came in, well sponsored but not skilled. And he gave me only a satisfactory rating. And I was furious.

"I had cleaned up the shop, got the engineers in shape. They'd not had a black manager before. So I asked why the rating wasn't as high as most of my previous ones. He said I stayed in the 'trench' too much. I wasn't visible. I should act like a sergeant, breathe down people's necks, let them know who's boss.

"I pointed out the improvements I'd made. Then I wrote a memo and said, 'You aren't recognizing what I've done. This place was a mess.' I could have grieved it formally, but I would have had to go to his boss and tell her what he did or didn't do.

She would have been angry at me for criticizing someone she had handpicked.

"People are polarized here. Many go to all-black churches. They went to all-black schools, have only black friends, and are suspicious of black people who live integrated lives, like mine.

"Our division is often invited to receptions and parties given by the corporations we do business with. I've asked my boss why he never goes, and he says, 'I don't feel comfortable.'

"We've got to get beyond this Amos and Andy Taxicab Company b.s. Too many of us don't socialize interracially. And black managers try to make me justify why I have white friends. The parochialism among black business and professional people is a problem.

"There's no way I could ever fit into the upper black circles here, because I'm not affiliated with the right social, civic, and fraternal groups. I'm not visible in the black circles. And, I'm Catholic. And the church I go to is predominately white. People even say, 'Why not go to Saint D's instead?'—the main black Catholic church. But I'm just not the type that would fit into the black management and professional circuit in this city. So it turns out, ironically, I'm evaluated by blacks on suitability and not passing the test.

"I'm a good manager. But they discount that because of the social thing. The black power network is powerful, and it matters. These tendencies lead blacks in authority to fail to recognize and use talented subordinate blacks. But if the group is so limited in its thinking, I don't want to be part of it anyway.

"People get promoted here for seeming to work hard, but not really doing the job. This organization needs tightening up. And the sad part is, most senior managers are black. But younger blacks coming in are better technically. And they don't refer to each other derogatively like the older ones. Mutual professional respect is getting higher. Blacks were hypercritical of each other."

Carl Cash

"Blacks come to me in trouble, and I've saved a few. When I couldn't, I've helped them go out with dignity. But some tried to use me, didn't tell me the whole story, and it turned out they were responsible for their bad situation. I've also intervened when I saw people getting shafted. But be careful. If you stick your neck out for blacks, be selective. Don't misuse your clout or you'll lose credibility. Pick your shots, and it enhances your overall credibility."

Ossie Gordon

"I go out of my way to spend time with the younger blacks in my firm. Go to lunch. Have an open door. Be available. It's important to cooperate and work together."

Cecil Clemens

"I've extended myself to blacks on my staff. I'm active in the National Association of Black Accountants. I got approval to use firm resources to support NABA. And I've urged our black staff to get involved. I reach out to black auditors and consultants as they come in. We have no formal organization, but we should. Some folks say that's risky. It will mark me as a potential rabble-rouser. But I'm solid professionally. And I don't worry. I don't violate protocol."

Bill Tompkins

"Here, we have mutual respect. But we're in different functions. Some have stronger relationships, some, nothing. But it's also culture and tradition. A black manager reports to me. And I do things socially with her. We have a good relationship. She would do anything to help me succeed. But a white manger who works for me also would. If they hadn't supported me as they do, I'd be in deep trouble. Two others in the division, I have no relationship with. Another senior black guy went out of his way to back me when I came in. He said, 'There are so few, we have to help each other.' "

Pam Stetson, 48, is a senior manager in municipal government.

"I've seen unbelievable turf wars in organizations with black leadership, public and private sector. But I get along and avoid arguments at all costs.

"Blacks are uneven. Some competent. Some bumbling fools. Managers are viewed based on quality of staff. I had nine lawyers. I hired two, but they all reflected on me. Some were marginal. They did the minimum to get a satisfactory rating, but they were not committed. And I doubt they would have responded differently to a white supervisor. Some people half-step in black organizations because they think they can get away with it. But they cheat themselves and others."

Alan Roland

"Whites are uncomfortable with too many blacks, and that influences how we behave. It's like when we move into a neighborhood. One is acceptable. In fact, one is preferable to none. Two is okay. But three, four or five—that's different. And that affects how we treat each other."

Earl Newsome

"How we get along depends on whether we're about the task or about feelings. We work well together if we're task-oriented. Working with black colleagues, two things happen. Some are dubious about you, if you're good, because your success refutes their lack of it. If you succeed, it says to them, 'He's doing okay.' So either it's not all that racist here, or he's really better than I am.' And if they conclude the latter, they have to face themselves.

"Working with black subordinates can be tricky, too. They may ask for understanding. They may resent you. They may try to get personal, and that can neutralize your leadership.

"What you do depends on who you are. I stay task-oriented and deal one on one with people. As a manager, you don't have a special squeeze with black employees. They may expect you to understand their plight. But that can interfere with accomplishing tasks and send a signal to white employees that's destructive. So be aware of whites' reactions. They often try to create conflict. And they like to see blacks paired off. 'Do you think so and so is arrogant?' That kind of question. I say something positive instead. Don't get drawn in, because if you say something negative, it will be used against both of you."

Helen Ellis

"Deal person to person. I've seen very destructive scenarios. Me First, Whatever the Consequences. But it would be glorious to identify with each other and pull together. As a consultant, I've had blacks in client companies take me aside and try to help me get the contract or compete an assignment. But I've seen black people go out of their way to block me from access, to try to hold onto some power. They imply to their boss, 'I can take care of this for you. You don't need her.' So it's to increase their value to their company. But it's also based on personal chemistry, and personality fit."

Ben Allison

"We have a companywide black organization. But staff blacks at headquarters don't identify with the folks at division, regional, or branch level. Most have been here ten, twenty years, surviving and succeeding, and have a shell that's hard to penetrate by appealing to racial identification. You can't assume that someone with the same paint job shares the same values. That's been an education for me."

Mode 3

Adam Compton, 40, is an engineering manager in a large aerospace firm.

"Here the black managers are close. Some go back to high school, and even to the old neighborhood and grade school. Every year, I have a barbecue for the blacks in the division. But I don't measure myself by the 'black' standard. I compete against everybody. So don't feel jealous when other blacks do better."

Larry Prince

"At the bank, the president was black. I've never had a better time. He's a unique personality. Anybody would like to work for him. I had great success and cooperation because people perceived I had his support.

"Later, at the foundation, I got some touching notes from other blacks. There was an alliance among black officers. But once, I called a guy, and he didn't return calls. I got pissed and stormed into his office. When I saw he was black, I cussed him out. Then we became friends.

"Some blacks deliberately avoid group participation. They're afraid it marks them as black first in loyalty and orientation. They don't want to signal that we're conspiring or clannish. But we can organize and cooperate without threatening. The sense that there will only be one black VP leads to exaggerated rivalries. Just do your best. Excel for its own sake. Companies shouldn't set up situations that pit blacks against each other. But they do. Don't let yourself be pigeonholed. Let management know we're candidates for all jobs, not just 'black VP.'

"Whites will talk to you about another black's performance. Cut that off. Nip it in the bud."

Bob Evans, 55, teaches at a major university and worked in senior management in nonprofits.

"I was a candidate for a major job in a civic association. I went to seek advice from important senior blacks in our city, old friends of mine. One said, 'Go for it.' The other didn't think I was right for the job. Later, I found both had supported a white candidate. Why weren't they straight with me? Why do folks do this? I trusted them. Black people have got to stop this. But I still don't know all the reasons. Maybe there were circumstances that explain it. But this is too common, and it undermines our ability to work together, trust, get things done, and evaluate each other.

"Now I'm paranoid about other prominent blacks and wonder whether I can trust. This is terrible. We have to back each other, not backstab."

Jack Davidson

"We have to get beyond the idea that security and high salary are what we're after. That isn't enough. Entrepreneuring, building something independently, should be what we're after. I see black professionals less willing to settle for comfort. But distrust and low confidence among blacks slows our process. I do deals based on close personal relationships with people who are good at what they do and comfortable with who they are. They know they'll be okay no matter how the deal turns out. They're willing to risk.

"We're looking at a deal where we have longstanding ties, been through similar wars, are comfortable with each other, respect each other's technical ability. The chemistry is right. I almost did a deal with a classmate. But in the end, we were different types of people. Social class among blacks helps determine how they match. That's tough to face. But background compatibility matters, not just race.

"The people I'm working with have been to the best schools, where they got the idea they were destined to impact on the world. They built confidence. But other black folks, with different backgrounds, often continue to doubt themselves.

"At the consulting firm, blacks were supportive, and if anyone could do something for you, he'd do it. That's happening more, and I'm glad. We need that. There's been too much backstabbing.

"The two black officers at our major client have given me resistance, but the whites have been tremendously helpful. It's the same old jealousy. One tried to throw a contract out that had been approved by the program officers, the direct client, on a two-dollar technicality.

"I've had white officers bend over backwards to help us, because they knew we were good, could help them, and wanted their project to work. And that meant hiring us. But when we get second- and third-generation decision makers in these jobs, with different perceptions of who they are, it will change.

"Downsizing is positive because it means you have to *produce*. There won't be many token slots left. So go into bottom-line jobs rather than traditional token slots."

13

Helping the Community

"It's difficult to believe that people are starving in this country because food isn't available."

RONALD REAGAN

"Everybody can be great because everybody can serve."

MARTIN LUTHER KING JR.

"Compassion is not weakness, and concern for the unfortunate is not socialism."

HUBERT H. HUMPHREY

"Don't stop 'til you get enough."

QUINCY JONES

You're in management to cause change. If you weren't expected to help reform businesses, then why would African Americans, in general, care whether you got in and moved ahead? Your personal success is nice, but it's expected that you will make a difference that will have broader consequences.

It's difficult to change organizations no matter what your level. It's especially hard when you're at relatively lower or middle levels of management, with enough problems just doing your job. But you're nevertheless expected to move the organization incrementally in progressive directions.

You can be a force for internal change, for example, with regard to EEO and affirmative action and black business investment and contracting and procurement. You don't have to be a specialist in those fields to notice bias in procedures and to speak to the right managers about it.

Maynard Jackson, speaking to a business group, put it well: "Money alone cannot save us. We don't have enough time to put into place economic institutions to save our people. It requires business and politics. Politics is not perfect, but it is the best available nonviolent means of changing how we live.... Don't get power, knowledge, and wisdom and then be afraid to use them. White America expects you to use your power for your people."

That's debatable, of course. Old Boys and Yammies expect you to try to create change. But they'll also work to nullify changes that would draw on corporate resources or use corporate leverage for causes you espouse.

What you can strive to do, though, is use your position and influence to directly or indirectly help improve external conditions. Mentor, reach back, and remember that each one can teach one. And you can work with managers you trust to bring about internal reforms in policy and practice that will benefit external constituencies.

What You Can Do

Recognize the Leverages of "Relations" Jobs

First, let's deal with a common misperception. We often hear complaints about tokenism. The theme is that public affairs, community relations, EEO, government relations, etc., are out of the mainstream, dead-end token slots, that they're cut disproportionately in downsizings, and that companies easily decide to de-emphasize them.

There's no need to lament the downsizings. Instead recognize that the programs have great leverage if used creatively. And we need to come up with innovative ways to make them successful as change agents.

If you're in a "relations" job, you have skills and experience that are valuable. For historic reasons black managers are still disproportionately few in those functions. If you're in such a staff job, make it a point to read all the mainstream business press— *Forbes, Business Week, Fortune,* the *Wall Street Journal,* and *Harvard Business Review*—that general line managers read. Also read the journals in marketing and financial and operations management so that your thinking and perspective remain mainstream business.

The real trouble is not that these are staff jobs. Obviously, these are important, rewarding, even crucial functions. They deserve respect and support. The trouble is that they tend to become overloaded with marginal performers and to be used politically as sinecures, patronage posts, and way stations. That's partly the fault of people in these jobs who let themselves become appendages, losing track of the point of the overall enterprise. Look for ways to add value. If you do, you'll be more effective and satisfied in using the tools available for meaningful change.

Help Individually and Collectively

Surveys suggest that young black managers, so-called Buppies, are generally more conservative, more politically active, more distrustful of established black leaders, and more distrustful of whites in general than are most black people.

Thomas E. Cavanaugh, of the Joint Center for Political and Economic Studies, finds that Buppies are altruistic but also have a strong streak of self-interest that influences their views on public issues and helps determine how they use their position and influence for community purposes. They also feel that despite their relative success thus far, they're still in a precarious spot, and a bad turn of events or a nasty shift in social climate could undo much they've managed to achieve. So they are preoccupied with reinforcing their newly won gains. Joint Political Action Committees like the 21st Century Institute in Washington and the Progressive Alliance in Atlanta, or similar groups in many cities, are avenues they use to express themselves politically.

We often hear that the black middle class hasn't done enough to help solve the problems of those who are struggling in chronic distress. This charge frequently comes from those ignorant of internal development programs that have succeeded for over three hundred years. Self-help is nothing new. All that notwithstanding, the middle class is key to solving the problem over the next forty years.

You're fortunate, and your resources and skills can make a difference. Concentrate on education, housing, crime prevention, health, recreation, or employment training and business development. Find a program that can use your expertise. Help the Children's Defense Fund, NAACP, Urban League, United Negro College Fund, and all sorts of local and neighborhood groups. Work through your sorority, fraternity, lodge, or church. Be a Big Brother or Big Sister, or a Cub Scout, Girl Scout, or Boy Scout leader, or serve on the board of advisors or as a merit badge counselor.

Twenty-five percent of all black households are in the suburbs. The word *suburbs* is tricky, including older nearby urban communities that are really not what the word conjures up. Nonetheless, even allowing for the imprecision in the term, the black middle class has dispersed somewhat, and this means that helping those who are in the inner city may mean inconveniences and logistical expense.

It's fine for the black middle class to enjoy the lifestyle it chooses. But it's not all right for there to be such a void of institutions effectively linking middle class talents, contacts, and resources to overall community development. Your role is to help fill that void, directly or indirectly, actively or passively.

Michael Lomax, chairman of the Fulton County Commission in Atlanta, says, "I wouldn't want to accuse of being turncoats those who choose to exercise their economic option." But that implies that he does, indeed, feel that there's almost a kind of disloyalty to the race and to the community when upwardly mobile black professionals and managers opt out of the geographic confines of the traditional ghetto.

But such attitudes don't help us solve problems or accelerate development. People are going to move where they choose. The trick is to link them all into productive networks that accomplish the goal of economic growth for the poor and marginal in the cities and rural areas.

Too many of the prosperous seem to think they have the option of *not* contributing. As long as there's no clear and present danger, no threat of pogroms, disfranchisement, property confiscation, expulsion, deportation—all threats that racial minorities have experienced in the past in Western democratic societies, and that under the wrong circumstances could happen again—that point of view is understandable.

But it's more rational to behave according to an assumption that the black community is vulnerable to attack and that individual freedom could be threatened. Therefore, it's a matter of long-run self-interest to help build institutions and create protective organizations and social and political systems against the day when unforeseen adversaries might adopt such tactics.

This is not to use that overused and emotional term "survival." But it is to insist that black managers should be less casual about their obligation to contribute at least regular moneys to community development. That, and political allegiance, are minimum.

The Business Exchange is a support group of black executives. It's the kind of instrument through which senior black managers can organize to effect change and coordinate their activities in community development.

You're more likely than Old Boys and Yammies to be in sympathy with corporate critics like Ralph Nader or the Interfaith Center on Corporate Responsibility, the Council on Economic

Priorities, and so on. But this tendency to be a critic of corporate international behavior in the Third World, of environmental practices, and of community stances, puts you at odds with prevailing company sentiment. And it reduces your leverage to help the community when you're seen as opposing the company's interest on sensitive social issues and lined up with these critics.

But we have a chance to help individuals in trouble. You can do it hands-on, one on one, face to face. You can also do it indirectly through contributions of time, talent, and money to organizations working on problems of health, housing, economic development, recreation, education, and so on.

The important thing to recognize is your obligation to use your resources—talent, power, contacts, budgets—to help accelerate community development. You can be bourgeois in style, taste, and social orientation. You can even be a Buppie and still have an impact. The point is not to waste time and energy pondering abstractions. Roll up your sleeves and contribute—or take out your checkbook and contribute. Not everyone has to be hands-on—as long as they are counted in the lists of important nondirect contributors financially, politically, intellectually, or organizationally.

The less fortunate, the underclass, the poor—whatever they're called in the media and by the pundits and pop analysts—the black community has many people who, for complex reasons, aren't yet able to feel secure and satisfied with their share. Developing their skills and bringing them into full participation is part of your obligation. It's in your self-interest, and it's an essential expression of soul in management.

Now let's sketch out a view of how to accelerate black community development. Then we'll consider how you, at any level in your company, can help the entire community as well as the specific communities you live and work in.

Two key organizations capable of accelerating development in African-American communities are the NAACP and the Urban League. They have a kind of quasi-public character. They speak for black people and are looked to by the general public, journalists, politicians, and business leaders for positions on issues. They are taken to represent mainstream black thinking. They're also important advocates and watchdogs.

But they have an opportunity—and obligation—to lead in economic development that they don't always follow through on. The problem is, they, along with other civil rights organizations, are still led by "civil rights leaders." That was appropriate for several generations, but no longer. Civil rights leaders are typically trained in law, journalism, social work, politics, the ministry, or the academic behavioral sciences. Their habits of mind, generally, are to look for solutions outside the community—the courts, legislatures, the press and public opinion, government agencies, foundations, the Fortune 500, and the Almighty. All those are still worth cultivating as allies. But the talent, strength, imagination, and resources we need for development are primarily internal, not external. Black people have the tools they need to accomplish most of what needs to be done.

The leaders needed, therefore, will have casts of mind that first think of ways to mobilize and galvanize resources within the black community. They should have a *managerial* point of view. We need leaders trained and experienced in modern management in corporate or government settings. Procter & Gamble, GM, IBM, McKinsey, Goldman Sachs, Chase Manhattan, Merrill Lynch, Arthur Anderson—organizations like these are where our leaders should come from.

The NAACP and Urban League are like troubled corporations. In the 1990s they have moved in the right directions, but they need help. You might even think of taking a one- or two-year full-time tour to work on community development as a paid staff manager in one of them.

Once on board, you can help them do the job that's needed. If the NAACP and Urban League can't do the job, then we need new organizations, unburdened by internal politics and personality. A national development corporation, perhaps, should be created. Or the National Black MBA Association's (NBMBAA) new thrust into development might turn out to be the right kind of vehicle.

Here is what the NAACP, the Urban League, or a national development corporation should emphasize. First, their development objective should be to reach income parity by the year 2020. That means black and white median incomes should be roughly the same by that date. Such a specific challenge is needed. If the target seems wrong, pick a different one, but be specific.

Second, a prime impediment to development is our own dysfunctional behavior. Crime impedes development. So do other forms of breakdown. Community and civil rights leaders have to take those on and overcome them.

They can use marketing tools, Madison Avenue, and persuasive communication to reinforce standards of behavior that are wholesome and constructive. Behavior problems are, in part, marketing problems, and they have marketing solutions. Managerial leaders will understand that intuitively and find solutions that work. Most people know right from wrong but need to be reminded. Crime, teenage pregnancy, and other self-destructive behavior *can* be changed through persuasion.

The NAACP and Urban League should lead in that positive persuasion campaign. They can draw on expertise to make the case in sophisticated ways. If we can sell consumer products—cars, beer, and aftershave—we can sell values.

Small business development and job generation in distressed areas won't happen until behavior improves. We used to believe the causes and effects were the other way around. Invest, create jobs, and crime will go down. In an ideal world, that might happen. But in the real world, with economic and political constraints, the goal is to shape up first. Then investment will occur and jobs will be created. The communities have to be perceived as safe first. And potential employees have to be seen as disciplined and well behaved.

Third, we can raise lots of money for development internally. We can supplement education, health, housing, recreation, retraining, child care, senior citizen care, and business capital formation. We can't do it all, but we have the collective income to do much more.

Fund-raising can be managed. For a start we can raise $200

million annually with no trouble and more later. It will take sophisticated marketing and administration. But it takes money to raise money. That's the first hurdle. So a joint foundation grant of $5 million, matched by $1 million from major black contributors—say, $10,000 each from a hundred sports, entertainment, and business figures—would launch a perpetual program of broad-based direct mail fund-raising aimed at four to eight million African-American households.

The seed money would buy computers, mailing lists, fund-raising expertise, and advertising, and generally launch the fund correctly. Previous fund-raising programs haven't worked well. Chicken dinners and benefits aren't the way. Often their basic appeal is misconceived. Beyond that, they lack start-up capital, professional talent, and the necessary point of view.

Financial independence won't be achieved, but we'll be on the right road. It could be spearheaded by the NAACP and the Urban League or the NBMBAA.

Fourth, we're in an intellectual battle. We can be successful, but we haven't used the tools. We need several first-rate journals of analysis to help form public opinion and public policy. The NAACP publishes the *Crisis,* and the Urban League puts out the *Urban League Review* and the annual *State of Black America.* All seem inadequate. (They need to be sharpened and well used.) But great editors are needed. Leaders with a managerial point of view would see that and make it a priority.

Fifth, economic development should emphasize acquisitions, including leveraged buyouts, using creative public-private partnerships. We can encourage business start-ups and entrepreneurship of larger and smaller firms and in manufacturing and services. But to accelerate competitive small businesses, the NAACP and Urban League should concentrate, through for-profit and nonprofit subsidiaries and in other ways, on stimulating systematic acquisitions.

Sixth, and finally, the idea of reparations—the restitution principle—is key to the debate on public policy. The NAACP and Urban League can refine and advance this concept of redistributive justice.

This summary strategy for accelerating community development will help us move beyond inertia and leader bashing toward development. African-American managers can step forward in many ways and at many levels to help, addressing any one of these issues. Or they can look at the issues in some other way entirely. Whatever is the case, African-American managers are in a position to help solve chronic community distress and accelerate development, goals that will benefit all of us in concrete ways and enrich our souls.

The Modes and How They View Helping the Community

Mode 1 managers say the job is to concentrate on helping the company make profits. The pursuit of individual career objectives is their other paramount concern. Being a change agent is not part of the agenda and, in fact, is seen as highly risky and often as disloyal. They see a community role in terms of voluntarism only—helping with worthy projects—and are highly risk-averse, avoiding controversial activities scrupulously.

Mode 2 managers say it's fine to help the community from the corporate platform, but confrontations are to be avoided, and nothing should be done that will interfere with harmonious team relations or imply different priorities. But they go so far as to help organize collective actions intended to pressure decision makers, public and private, into policy and operating reforms.

Mode 3 managers say helping change is one of the main reasons for being there. They speak for change at every opportunity and use position and resources to help outside groups, including those critical of the company. They also are active in working to build permanent institutions that will carry on development and serve as countervailing forces against established institutions. They tend to carry on a "progressive" agenda derived from 1960s community-based models.

Mode 1

Cecil Clemens

"I use the firm's resources to help the community. I got them to donate a thousand dollars to the Coalition for the Homeless. The firm provides release time to be on these boards. And at our billing rates, that's significant. I'm on the Ministries United board. We rehab houses. And I'm on the board of Family Services. The firm values these pro bono activities. They urge me to get involved. And I'm chairing the group rehabing the Y.

Lou Benson

"I'm on General Hospital's board. I sponsor a Little League team in the housing project. And I teach for free at the university, at eight A.M., twice a week. My firm is supportive.

"One lady said, 'I notice you come to the projects in a BMW with a telephone, and bought uniforms for us. At first, I thought you were a drug dealer.' I laughed, then I thought, 'I bet some kids think that still.' So I took them for lunch at my office, so they'd see black people in accounting and consulting.

"Reach out this way. But some younger blacks think the way to make an impression in the firm is to give a lot of attention to outside activities. That's not how it works. Concentrate on building your internal reputation and being a technical asset. Then use firm time and resources for community projects. Be accountants and auditors first, not social workers. Older people who have made partner have to do more outside. But I still do most of it on my own time."

Ben Collins

"I've tried to get the bank into new activities. Advertise in black newspapers and support community programs. But they've only helped with a tutoring program. I've introduced candidates for jobs and given advice on minority personnel issues, although they have a full-time human resources officer for that."

Mode 2

Carl Cash

"I'm on the minority affairs committee of our trade association in advertising and marketing. But the whole industry has
trouble doing social projects because there's really no effective
support network for the people who care. If I make VP, I will
have clout in the company, the community, and the industry. I'll
be on industry committees.

"If the company places activist blacks in key jobs, it's seen as
a time bomb, because they're afraid they'll use the job to try to
change policy and practice. So I hate to say it, but you have to
play the game. Your priority, at least outwardly, has to be the
same as those at the top. You have to emphasize profits and the
status quo in order to be accepted. You can't emphasize that you
want to make changes. You have to get promoted first. Then
when you have power, you can quietly use it, carefully.

"I went to a senior management conference where a
B-school professor said that blacks who make it will be just like
whites. They'll live in the same areas, join the same clubs, vote
the same, and so on. They'll be no different. Senior managers
espouse the philosophy of the company. That's how they get to
be senior managers. But if you signal early that you want to
make changes, you'll be blocked, no matter how great your
performance.

"Unfortunately, blacks who've made it are not sufficiently involved in black causes, they tend to shun the spotlight, because
they know what that kind of visibility can do to hurt them. A
guy who becomes president of a black organization is setting
himself up. It's too high a profile. It will be seen as a threat.

"You need to concentrate on your job and be a quiet sup-
porter. Help out with community things. Serve on committees,
but don't be a leader. That's a huge difference. Allocate your
time wisely. Don't be a visible threat.

"We need more skilled mainstream people keeping the channels of communication open from the inside to activists on the

outside. That's why I live in D.C. rather than in the Maryland or Virginia suburbs—it's a statement of what I believe in. And it's a subtle yet nonthreatening signal to the company.

Henry Clapton

"In some ways, speaking out on social and political issues, inside and outside, protects you. But do a good basic job or your activism won't count."

Sam Claridge, 37, is a management consultant in a major consulting firm.

"We're effective at reform here because we understand the mentality and can communicate. There are many ways to fight the system. Companies are different. Here we're decentralized, so pressure on headquarters—for instance, for college recruiting or philanthropic donations to charities and community projects—doesn't produce much. So we leaned on the divisions."

Mode 3

Carl Battle, 37, is a lawyer for a chemical manufacturer.

"I can fulfill my obligation to blacks through involvement with youth and politics. But many of these middle-class blacks try to assimilate by abdicating their blackness. These people aren't concerned about the people they leave behind, only about money and succeeding in the white establishment."

Bob York

"I push for using minority contractors and hiring. Some people feel I'm a pain in the ass. And lately I've backed off of confrontation and tried persuasion."

Ralph Adams

"At the consulting firm, I drafted a statement of concerns—affirmative action hiring and promotion, criteria for taking on engagements such as in South Africa and for U.S. firms doing business there. Most of the black professionals signed, and I hand-carried it to the CEO's office. It probably helped change internal personnel policy, but not external business practices or client relationships. It was risky. The CEO had been anti-union in his earlier days in manufacturing, and he saw employee organizing, even professionals, as a threat."

A Final Word

We are optimistic about the future for African Americans in management. We know there are hurdles and anxiety, but the glass is more than half full.

Over the years a number of our colleagues have offered various perspectives on the progress and obstacles facing you. John Fernandez, Roosevelt Thomas, Ed Jones, and George Davis and Glegg Watson have helped greatly to illuminate the territory. They used various analytical modes in arriving at useful conclusions. We expect our work to stand with theirs and with others' to help ease the way and clear the path.

We have emphasized leadership and the political, psychological, and even spiritual dimension of life in the corporation. These new angles reflect the fact that African Americans have succeeded in gaining entry and establishing a broad record of success. The task for the next twenty years is to consolidate gains, embark on personal growth and the road to increased self-awareness, and learn to be effective managers while enjoying a multidimensional life with many sources of satisfaction.

SELECT BIBLIOGRAPHY

Books

Agor, Weston H. *Intuitive Management*. New York: Prentice Hall, 1984.

Baldwin, Bruce. *It's All In Your Head*. New York: Directions Dynamics, 1993.

Block, Peter. *The Empowered Manager*. San Francisco: Jossey-Bass, 1987.

Bradford, David L., and Allan R. Cohen, *Managing for Excellence*. New York: Wiley, 1984.

Davis, George, and Glegg Watson. *Black Life in Corporate America*. New York: Doubleday, 1982.

Deal, Terrence E., and Allen A. Kennedy. *Corporate Cultures*. Reading, Mass: Addison-Wesley, 1982.

Delany, William A. *Tricks of the Managers Trade*. New York: AMACOM, 1982.

Fernandez, John A. *Managing a Diverse Workforce*. Lexington, Mass. Lexington Books, 1991.

Fernandez, John P. *Survival in the Corporate Fishbowl*. Lexington, Mass: D.C. Heath, 1987.

Fisher, Roger, and William Ury. *Getting to Yes*. Boston: Houghton Mifflin, 1981.

Freeman, Sue M. *Managing Lives: Corporate Women and Social Change*. Amherst: University of Massachusetts, 1990.

Grieff, Barry S., and Preston K. Munter. *Tradeoffs*. New York: Mentor, 1981.

Grove, Andrew. *High Output Management*. New York: Random House, 1985.

Heclo, Hugh. *A Government of Strangers*. Washington, D.C.: Brookings, 1977.

Helgeson, Sally. *The Female Advantage: Women's Ways of Leadership*. New York: Doubleday, 1990.

Herman, Stanley M., and Michael Korenich. *Authentic Management*. Reading, Mass: Addison-Wesley, 1977.

Hummel, Ralph P. *The Bureaucratic Experience*. New York: St. Martin's Press, 1977.

Kanter, Rosabeth Moss. *The Change Masters*. New York: Simon and Schuster, 1983.

Kennedy, Marilyn Moats. *Office Politics*. Chicago: Follett, 1980.

Kotter, John P. *The General Managers*. New York: Free Press, 1982.

Leavitt, Harold J. *Corporate Pathfinders*. Homewood, Ill: Dow-Jones Irwin, 1986.

Maccoby, Michael. *The Gamesman*. New York: Simon and Schuster, 1976.

_____. *The Leader*. New York: Ballantine, 1981.

Naisbett, John and Patricia Aburdene. *Reinventing the Corporation*. New York: Warner, 1985.

Nierenberg, Gerard, I. *The Art of Negotiating*. New York: PB, 1989.

O'Toole, James. *Vanguard Management*. New York: Berkley, 1985.

Ouchi, William G. *Theory Z*. Reading, Mass: Addison-Wesley, 1981.

Pascal, Richard, and Anthony Athos. *The Art of Japanese Management*. New York: Simon and Schuster, 1981.

Peters, Thomas J., and Robert H. Waterman, Jr. *In Search of Excellence*. New York: Harper and Row, 1982.

Peters, Tom. *Liberation Management*. New York: Knopf, 1992.

Peters, Tom, and Nancy Austin. *A Passion for Excellence*. New York: Random House, 1985.

Sargent, Alice G. *The Androgynous Manager*. New York: AMACOM, 1981.

Senge, Peter M. *The Fifth Discipline*. New York: Doubleday, 1990.

Skinner, C. Wickham. *Manufacturing*. New York: Wiley, 1985.

Thomas, R. Roosevelt, Jr. *Beyond Race and Gender*. New York: AMACOM, 1991.

Thompson, Paul, and Gene Dalton. *Novations*.

Townsend, Robert. *Up the Organization*. New York: Knopf, 1977.

_____. *Further Up the Organization*. New York: Knopf, 1984.

Walton, Mary. *The Deming Management Method*. New York: Putnam, 1986.

White, Marjorie, and Marcella Wiener. *The Theory and Practice of Self-Psychology*. New York: Brunner-Mazel, 1986.

Wilson, James Q. *Bureaucracy*. New York: Basic Books, 1989.

Periodicals

Aplin-Brownlee, Vivian, "Blacks and Whites Still Talk To Each Other Through Masks," *Washington Post*.

Archer, Frank W., "Charting a Career Course," *Personnel Journal*, April 1984, 60–64.

Argyris, Chris, "The CEO's Behavior. Key to Organizational Development," *Harvard Business Review*, March–April 1972, 55–64.

Baldwin, Bruce A., "What You Think Is What You Get," *Piedmont Airlines Magazine*, October 1985, 11.

Binzen, Peter, "With Varied Traits but a Common Drive," *Philadelphia Inquirer*, February 27, 1984.

_____, "A New Commandment for Managers," *Philadelphia Inquirer*, April 9, 1984.

"Black Football Coaches Are Down to Zero in Division 1-A," *Philadelphia Inquirer*, June 1, 1992. This article suggests that some occupations and some industries present special barriers. The article quotes Ron Dickerson, hired in late 1992 as Temple University's head coach and president of the Black

Coaches Association, as saying he's thinking of writing a book to be titled "Not Qualified."

Blonston, Gary, "Blacks Face Dilemmas As More Move to the Suburbs," *Philadelphia Inquirer*, August 25, 1986, p. 1.

Bolick, Clint, "Blacks and Whites on Common Ground," *Wall Street Journal*, August 5, 1992. A conservative suggests that the Republican Party has failed to attract blacks because of "years of hostility or neglect by Republicans toward matters of concern to black Americans."

Brown, Tom, "Match Up With a Mentor," *Industry Week*, October 1, 1990, 18.

Bulkeley, William M., "The Fast Track: Computers Help Firms Decide Whom to Promote," The Wall Street Journal.

Burhoff, Barbara, "Excuses, Excuses, Excuses," *Washington Post*, March 3, 1986.

Byrne, John A., "Is Your Company Too Big?, *Business Week*, March 27, 1989, 84–94.

———, "Nuts and Bolts Bosses," *Forbes*, September 26, 1983, 128–30.

———, "The New Headhunters," *Business Week*, February 6, 1989, 64–71.

———, "Business Fads: What's In—What's Out," *Business Week*, January 20, 1986, 52–61.

———, "Be Nice to Everybody," *Forbes*, November 5, 1984.

Clayton, Janet, "Buppies: New Power in Politics, *Los Angeles Times*, August 26, 1985.

Corseri, Gary, "New Hiring Bias: White Men Last," *Philadelphia Inquirer*, April 22, 1992. This article offers a clear statement of resentment at affirmative action and diversity programs and the costs they are seen to impose on white men.

Day, Charles R., Jr., "Dejection and Resignation in the Ranks," *Industry Week*, December 8, 1986, p. 57.

Diamond, David, "Don't Hide in the Ladies Room," *Philadelphia Inquirer*, February 6, 1983.

Dimeo, Jean, "Promoting Cultural Diversity at Fannie Mae," *Washington Post*, August, 1992.

Drucker, Peter F., "Playing in the Information-Based Orchestra," *Wall Street Journal*, June 4, 1985.

Dumaine, Brian, "Creating a New Company Culture," *Fortune*, January 15, 1990, 127–31.

Epstein, Richard A., "Diversity Yes—but Without Coercion," *Wall Street Journal*, April 22, 1992. This article expresses the resentment that diversity is promoted by law rather than by individual choice of firms seeking competitive advantage in the marketplace.

"Executive Qualities," *HBS Bulletin*, May-June 1975.

Farnham, Alan, "Holding Firm on Affirmative Action," *Fortune*, March 13, 1989, pp. 87, 88.

———, "The Trust Gap," *Fortune*, December 4, 1989, 56–78.

Flanagan, William G., and Maria Fisher, "Out of the Foxholes," *Forbes*, January 2, 1984.

Flanigan, William G., and Janet Bamford, "More Than a Moving Experience," *Forbes*, November 21, 1983, 310–12.

Fowler, Elizabeth M., "Counseling Dismissed Managers," *New York Times*, September 26, 1984.

Gemmill, Gary, and Donald DeSilva, "The Promotion Beliefs of Managers As a Factor in Career Progress," *Sloan Management Review*, Winter, 1977.

Gite, Lloyd, Building a Winning Staff, *Black Enterprise*, July 1984.

Gittler, Harvey, "Time to Honor Middle Managers," *Industry Week*, September 3, 1990, p. 30.

———, "Therapy for Neurotic Organizations," *Across the Board*, March 1985.

Goleman, Daniel, "The Strange Agony of Success," *New York Times*, August 24, 1986.

Goodman, Ellen, "Love at Work Is a Dangerous Game," *Washington Post*, September 27, 1983.

Green, Connie, "From Roadblocks to Rapport: Understanding Your Boss," *Black Enterprise*, June 1984.

Half, Robert, *Forbes*, October 15, 1990, 212–14.

Harris, Marilyn A., "What Keeps IBM, 'So Big, So Square, So True'?," *Business Week*, January 20, 1986.

Hodge, Sally Saville, "The Office Grapevine," *San Francisco Examiner and Chronicle*, August 28, 1983.

———, "More Workers at All Levels Unhappy With Jobs," *Philadelphia Daily News*, October 17, 1983.

"How Spouses Influence Executives," *Business Week*, May 2, 1983.

Hussein, Mohamed El Mutassin, "The Presence of a 'Third Culture' in a Western Society," *Human Resource Management*, Spring 1981, 31–33.

Hymowitz, Carol, "More Managers Try Moonlighting to Boost Income and Fulfillment," *Wall Street Journal*, August 9, 1983.

Jaffe, Henry, "Best 100: Firms That Offer Workers the Right Stuff," *Washington Post*, April 30, 1984.

Johnson, Kirk, "Why References Aren't, 'Available on Request,' " *New York Times*, June 5, 1985.

Johnson, Terry E., "Debating a Debt: What Do Blacks Who Prosper Owe the Rest?," *Philadelphia Inquirer*, May 19, 1985.

Jones, Alex S., "Editors Take on Conflicts of News Staff Diversity," *New York Times*, April 9, 1992.

"Keep Employees Informed," *Small Business Report*, June 1983.

Keidel, Robert W., "A New Game Plan for Managers to Play," *New York Times*, December 8, 1985.

Kennedy, Joyce Lain, "Negotiating the Twists and Turns on the Road to Success," *Philadelphia Inquirer*, February 9, 1986.

Kiechel, Walter, III, "The Neglected Art of Career Planning," *Fortune*, June 27, 1983, 153–55.

———, "Asking for a Raise," *Fortune*, January 19, 1984.

———, "Resurrecting Corporate Loyalty," *Fortune*, December 9, 1985.

———, "No Word From On High," *Fortune*, January 6, 1986.

———, "How to Take Part in a Meeting," *Fortune*, March 26, 1986.

———, "When a Headhunter Calls," *Fortune*, May 8, 1989, 161.

Kinkead, Gwen, "On a Fast Track to the Good Life," *Fortune*, April 7, 1980, 74–83.

Kipnis, David, and Stuart Schmidt, "The Power of Persuasion," *Washington Post*, July 19, 1985.

Korn, Lester B., "How the Next CEO Will Be Different," *Fortune*, May 22, 1989, pp. 157–161.

Kotlowitz, Alex, and Suzanne Alexander, "The Gulf, Tacit Code of Silence on Matters of Race Perpetuates Divisions, Blacks Tend to Be Reluctant to Share Experiences; Whites Often Shun Topic," *Wall Street Journal*, May 28, 1992.

Kovacevich-Costello, Genita, "How to Decide If You're Suited to a Big or a Small Firm," *San Jose Mercury News*, July 3, 1983.

Kristie, James, "Nothing Succeeds Like Excellence," *Philadelphia Inquirer*, June 2, 1985.

Labich, Kenneth, "Making Over Middle Managers," *Fortune*, May 8, 1989, pp. 58–64.

LaBier, Douglas, "Madness Stalks the Ladder Climbers," *Fortune*, September 1, 1986, 79.

Laskey, Alice Urbansky, "Knowing How You Deal With Conflict Is the Key to Success in Negotiation," *Philadelphia Inquirer*, March 16, 1986.

Lefferts, Nicholas E., "What's New in Corporate Alumni Groups," *New York Times*, June 9, 1985.

Lorie, James H., "Ten Steps to Wonderland," *Wall Street Journal*, September 19, 1985.

Lynch, Frederick R., "Multiculturalism Comes to the Workplace," *Wall Street Journal*, October 26, 1992.

Machan, Dyan, "The Charisma Merchants," *Forbes*, January 23, 1989, 100–101.

———, "The Clients Are Restless," *Forbes*, July 10, 1989, 114–17.

———, "How to Aim High," *Forbes*, November 12, 1992, 348–49.

Maccoby, Michael, "The Executive Suite," *Washington Post*, January 9, 1983.

Magnet, Myron, "Managing by Mystique at Tandem Computers," *Fortune*, June 28, 1982.

Main, Jeremy, "Look Who Needs Outplacement," *Fortune*, October 9, 1989, 85–92.

McDowell, Jerome Dorin, "Joy Loyalty. Not the Virtue It Seems, *New York Times*, March 3, 1985.

McKenna, Joseph F., "The Bounties of Mutiny—Can Management Use Job Hopping to the Company's Advantage?" *Industry Week*, May 7, 1990, 11–13.

———, "Looking For and Building a Few Good Heroes," *Industry Week*, October 15, 1990, 16–19.

"The Megatrends Man," *Newsweek*, September 1985, 58–61.

Mesdag, Lisa Miller, "Are You Underpaid?" *Fortune*, March 19, 1984, 20–25.

Moore, Michael L., and K. Dow Scott, "Installing Management By Objectives in a Public Agency: A Comparison of Black and White Managers, Supervisors and Professionals," *Public Administration Review*, March 1983, 121–29.

Nelson, Bryce, "The Drive to Get Even: Why People Try to Suppress Their Desire for 'Sweet Revenge,' " *Washington Post*, December 16, 1986.

O'Reilly, Brian, "Is Your Company Asking Too Much?" *Fortune*, March 12, 1990, 38–46.

Oldenburg, Don, "Putting Your Best Foot Forward," *Washington Post*, May 20, 1985.

——, "The Bottom Line Is Laughter," *Washington Post*, March 4, 1986.

Peters, Tom, and Nancy Austin, "A Passion for Excellence," *Fortune*, May 12, 1985.

Poe, Randall, "Paying the Bill for Job Stress," *Washington Post*, February 20, 1987, B5.

Pollock, Ellen Joan, and Milo Geyelin, "Many Black Lawyers in Elite Law Firms Feel They Don't Fit In, Survey Shows," *Wall Street Journal*, May 12, 1992. This reports a survey that found younger Asian and Hispanic lawyers felt less hostility, estrangement, and differentness than comparable African Americans.

Pope, Leroy, "What to Do to Motivate Executives," *Philadelphia Bulletin*, October 31, 1977.

Porter, Sylvia, "Don't Make Job Move Without Testing Self," *Washington Post*, November 24, 1981.

Posner, Barry Z., and Warren A. Schmidt, "Determining Managerial Strategies in the Public Sector," *Human Resource Management*, Summer 1982.

Raizada, Vishist K. Vaid, "Multi-ethnic Corporations and Inter-ethnic Conflict," *Human Resources Management*, Fall 1981, 24–27.

Rigdon, Joan E., and Carol Hymowitz, "For Black Men, Success Resolves Few Problems," *Wall Street Journal*, August 9, 1992.

Rubin, Sylvia, "How to Cope With Difficult People," *San Francisco Chronicle*, August 19, 1983.

Scanlon, Susan, "The Way You Were and Are," *Washington Post*, May 23, 1983.

Sifford, Darrell, "How to Answer Questions Asked at the Job Interview," *Philadelphia Inquirer*, June 19, 1984.

——, "What to Do If What the Boss Says Doesn't Make Sense," *Philadelphia Inquirer*, April 25, 1985.

——, "Feedback: The Necessary Ingredient for Leadership," *Philadelphia Inquirer*, January 27, 1986.

——, "The Corporate Romance: Can It Be Made to Work?" *Philadelphia Inquirer*, April 3, 1986.

——, "You And Your Boss: Take Charge of That Relationship," *Philadelphia Inquirer*, February 16, 1987.

——, "A Self-Defense Guide for the Corporate Battleground," *Philadelphia Inquirer*.

Smart, William, "Corporate Creativity," *Washington Post*, March 12, 1984.

Solman, Paul, and Thomas Friedman, "The MBA and the Decline of American Industry," *Washington Post*, August 8, 1982.

Swinyard, Alfred W., and Floyd A. Bond, "Who Gets Promoted," *Harvard Business Review*, September–October 1980.

Symonds, Bill, "You Got The Ax. Now What Should You Do?" *Business Week*, January 23, 1989, 110.

Torry, Saundra, "Here's Some Free Advice From Minority Lawyers," *Washington Post*, July 6, 1992. This is a typical article dealing with anecdotal evidence that many African-American professionals, in this case lawyers, feel alienated from their colleagues.

Wareham, John, "Keep Your Job in a Recession," *Inc.*, January 1980.

Wysocki, Bernard, Jr., "The Chief's Personality Can Have Big Impact for Better or Worse," *Wall Street Journal*, September 11, 1984.

Yenckel, James T., "Capitalizing On People." *Washington Post*, February 22, 1983.

_____, "Putting Your Best Presentation Forward," *Washington Post*, December 27, 1983.

_____, "Teaming Up for Success," *Washington Post*, March 5, 1984.

INDEX

Activism, 21–22, 110–11
Advancement. *See* Promotions
Affirmative action, xix
Ambivalents, 16
American Management Association (AMA), 138
Anger, 177–80
Anxiety, 179
Appraisals. *See* Performance appraisals
Appreciation, need for, 183
Art of Japanese Management, The (Athos & Pascal), 112
Art of Negotiating, The (Nierenberg), 118
Authoritarian managers, xv
Avoiders, 17

Bias in performance appraisals, 45–47
Black and White Styles in Conflict (Kochman), 180
Black Enterprise, x
Black managers, categorizing, 20–22, 94, 200. *See also* Mode types for black managers
Black managers, relationships between, 197–211
Boss, working with your, 60
    conflict resolution, 67–68
    credibility gaps, 66
    disagreements, 65–66
    impressing, 88
    mode types for black managers, 71–84
    mutual strengths/interests, 61
    respecting the relationship, 68–69
    role expectations, 62–63
    self-initiative, 64
    sizing up, 61
    sponsorship, 70–71
    starting a career, 32–34
Bosses, types of, 49
Brown, Jerry, 40
Buppies, 214–15
Bush administration, 141
Business Exchange, The, 216

Career paths, 7, 88, 91. *See also* Starting a career
Cavanaugh, Thomas E., 214
Ceilings (promotion barriers), 5, 94–95
Challenger, James E., 155
Change, being open to, 111–12
Colleagues
    socializing with 166–76
    white, 19–20, 63, 113, 115, 136, 151, 155–56
Collins, Eliza, 168
Command and control value systems, vii
Community, helping the. *See* Social change/justice
Companies
    critics of, 216–17
    cultures, ix–xi, 33, 151–52
    fast-growing, 179
    Fortune 1000, x–xi, 26
    slow-growing, 179–80
Conflict resolution, 67–68, 117–18, 152–53
Confrontation, 6–7, 65, 152–53, 180
Conservatism, 10
Coping With Difficult People (Bronson), 69
Corporate Cultures (Kennedy & Deal), 93, 151–52
Corporate Romance (Westoff), 167
Credibility, 66, 109, 197
Crime, 219

De Lorean, John Z., 108
DeSalvia, Donald, 86
Documentation and office politics, 150–51
Do It My Way or You're Fired: Employee Rights and the Changing Role of Management Prerogatives (Ewing), 68
Double standards, 11
Dressing for success, 89–90
Driver, Michael, 88
Drucker, Peter, 148
Dysfunctional behavior in black community, 219

233

Eason, Laras, 46
Economic development helping black
    community, 220
Education, continuing one's, 39
Emotions, managing
    anger and anxiety, 178–80
    coping skills, 177
    mid-life issues, 185–87
    mode types for black managers, 187–95
    Myer–Briggs Type Indicator, 182–83
    self-examination, 183–84
    stress, 180–82
    types of managers, 184–85
Executive Success (Jennings), 86
Employees, valued, 151

Failure, learning from, 99
Family Ties, Corporate Bonds (Bernstein),
    184
Feedback, 114
Financial independence, 39
Fortune 1000 firms, x–xi, 26
Fulfillment, sense of, 90
Fund-raising, 219–20
*Further Up the Organization: How to Stop
    Management From Stifling People and
    Strangling Productivity* (Townsend), 114

Game Plans: Sports Strategies for Business
    (Keidel), 112
Gamesman, The (Maccoby), 20
Gemmill, Gary, 86
General Motors, 46
Getting to Yes (Fisher & Ury), 118
Goals, achieving, 93–94, 109
Gossip, 153, 155
Grove, Andrew, 111

Half, Robert, 87
Headhunters (management recruiters),
    92–93, 95–97
High Output Management (Grove), 116
Hill, Norman J., 94
Honest, 153–55
Humor, sense of, 87, 117–18
Hussein, Mohamed, 137

Iacocca, Lee, 108
Individualistic leadership, 108
Injustice. *See* Social change/justice
Interpersonal skills, 33–34
Interviews, 97
Intuitive leaders, 111, 112
*It's All in Your Head: Lifestyle Management
    Strategies for Busy People* (Baldwin), 181

Job hopping, 89
Johnson, Lyndon, 152
Johnson, Wendell, 94
Journals analyzing black community, 220

Kanter, Donald, 69
Kanter, Rosabeth M., 168
Key to the Executive Head (Lerbinger &
    Sperber), 109

LaBier, Douglas, 184
Lateral organizations, 108, 109, 111,
    148–49
Layoffs, 49
Leadership, 107
    activism, 110–11
    change, being open to, 111–12
    community, helping the, 218, 220
    conflict resolution, 117–18
    effective, 109–10
    individualistic, 108
    lateral organizations, 149
    loyalty, 113–16
    meetings, running, 116–17
    mode types for black managers, 118–34
Leavitt, Harold, 36
Legalistic procedures and racism, 11
Life Orientation Outline (LIFO), 185
Literature on management, xvii
Lomax, Michael, 216
Loyalty, xi, xiv, 31, 113–16, 135, 136–47

Management styles, xv, 69, 111, 184–85.
    See also Mode types for black managers
Manners, 70
*Manufacturing: The Formidable Competitive
    Weapon* (Skinner), 112
McKee, Clarence, 198
Mechanistic productivity, 112
Meetings, running, 116–17
Middle class, black, 214–17
Middle managers, 111–12, 184
Mid-life issues, 185–87
Military service, 87
Mirvis, Philip, 69
Mobility and promotions, 90–92
Mode types for black managers
    black managers, relationships between,
        201–11
    boss, working with your, 71–84
    community, helping the, 221–25
    emotions, managing, 187–95
    leadership, 118–34
    loyalty, 139–47
    office politics, 156–65

performance appraisals, 50–59
promotions, 99–106
racism, view of, 22–25
realism mixed with optimism, 26–29
socializing with colleagues, 168–76
starting a career, 41–44
Moving Ahead: Black Managers in American Business (America & Anderson), viii
Myer-Briggs Type Indicator (MBTI), 182–83

Narcissistic managers, 184
National Association for the Advancement of Colored People (NAACP), 217–21
National Black MBA Association (NBMBAA), 218
Negotiation skills, 98–99, 118
Networking, 97, 200–201
Nine American Lifestyles (Mitchell), 110
Novations: Strategies for Career Development (Thompson), 91

Objectives, focusing on, 155
Obsessive managers, 184
Office politics, 150–53
  honest broker, being an, 153–55
  mode types for black managers, 156–65
  payback, wasting time on, 151
  practices involved, 149
Old Guard companies, vii, x, 5, 48, 61, 86, 108, 112
Organizational development, 48–49, 108, 109, 111, 148–49
Organization Man, The (Whyte), 86
O'Toole, James, x

Passion for Excellence, A (Peters & Austin), 111
Pepsico, 47
Performance appraisals
  bias, 45–47
  limitations of, 47–48
  mode types for black managers, 50–59
  participating in setting objectives, 48–49
  using, 49–50
Personality, 89
Planning, long-range, 88–89
Political parties, 139
Productivity, mechanistic, 112
Promotions
  ceilings, 94–95
  dressing for success, 89–90
  failure, learning from, 99
  foul ups, avoiding, 87
  goals, achieving concrete, 93–94

headhunters, 95–97
interviews, 97
loyalty, xiv, 140
mobility, 90–92
mode types for black managers, 99–106
negotiation skills, 98–99
philosophical compatibility, xi
plan, following a, 88
senior managers granting, 86–87
turning down, 92
Public managers, 110
Purgers (racism), 15
Pyramid Climbers (Packard), 86

Quality of management, 31

Race relations, 3–8
Racism, 9–29
  dictionary, 9–11
  institutional, 10
  levels of, 14–19
  mode types for black managers, 22–25
  performance appraisals, 46
  political background, understanding the, 24–25
Racists, working with, 12
Rage, 180
Rayburn, Sam, 152
Reagan administration, 141
Recruiters, management, 92–93, 95–97
Redistributive justice, 220–21
Reinventing the Corporation (Naisbett & Aburdene), 109
Relations jobs, 213–14
Resenters, 16–17
Retrogressives, 16
Rodgers, Buck, 63
Role expectations, 62–63
Romance at the office, 167–68
Rosofsky, Henry, 153
Rumsfeld, Donald, 66

Savvy scale, 22
Schizoid managers, 184
Secrecy, 115
Self-awareness, 179, 182, 183–84
Self-evaluation, 50
Self-initiative, 64
Self-interest, 4
Self-promotion, 93–94
Social change/justice, xii–xiii
  activism, 21–22, 110–11
  individual and collective help, 214–17
  loyalties, balancing, 136–37, 140–41
  misconceptions, dangerous, 5–7

mode types for black managers, 221–25
NAACP and Urban League, 217–21
relations jobs, 213–14
Socializing with colleagues, 166–76
Solids (white supporters), 18, 35, 47
Spirituality, 40–41
Sponsorship, 70–71
Starting a career
  analytical skills, 35–36
  correcting flaws, 33
  keys for, 30–31
  mode types for black managers, 41–44
  responsibility for development, 36–37
  satisfaction outside of job, 39–41
  standards for yourself, setting, 34–35
  volunteering, 37
  writing skills, 38
Status incongruence, 34, 108, 114
Stereotypes, living with, 38
Stevenson, Howard, 110
Stress, 180–82
Success, pressure to achieve, 183

Team play, xv, 152
Technical competence, 109

Theory and Practice of Self-Psychology, The
  (White & Wiener), 183
Theory Y and Z managers, xv
Third Culture concept, 137
Third Wave people, 63
Third World, 139
Thomas, Clarence, 141
Toffler, Alvin, 63
Tokenism, 213–14
Trivial concerns, avoiding, 112
Trust, 20, 65

Up the Organization (Townsend), 114
Urban League, 217–21

Valued employees, 151
Vanguard companies, ix–xi, 31, 47, 108,
  112, 113

Whites
  neutrals, 12–13, 15, 19
  racists, 12
  solids, 18, 35, 47
Wives of executives, 167
Writing skills, 38

DATE DUE

GAYLORD			PRINTED IN U.S.A